Skinny
Meals in
Heels

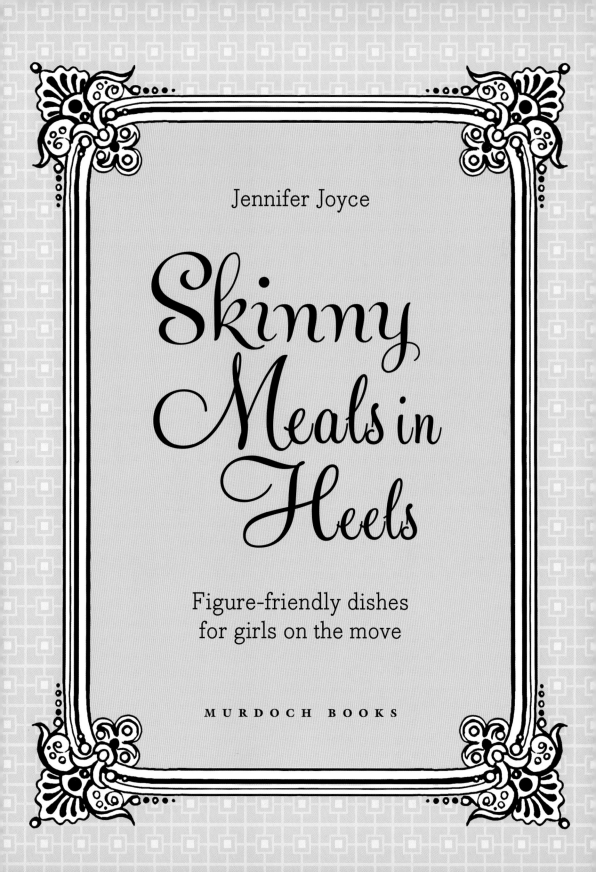

Jennifer Joyce

Skinny Meals in Heels

Figure-friendly dishes
for girls on the move

M U R D O C H   B O O K S

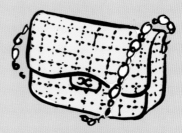

Contents

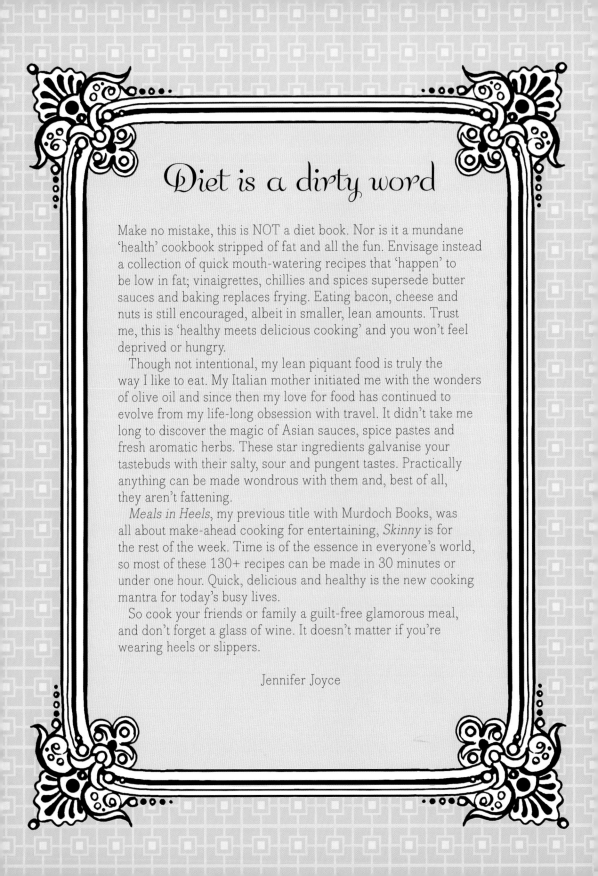

Diet is a dirty word

Make no mistake, this is NOT a diet book. Nor is it a mundane 'health' cookbook stripped of fat and all the fun. Envisage instead a collection of quick mouth-watering recipes that 'happen' to be low in fat; vinaigrettes, chillies and spices supersede butter sauces and baking replaces frying. Eating bacon, cheese and nuts is still encouraged, albeit in smaller, lean amounts. Trust me, this is 'healthy meets delicious cooking' and you won't feel deprived or hungry.

Though not intentional, my lean piquant food is truly the way I like to eat. My Italian mother initiated me with the wonders of olive oil and since then my love for food has continued to evolve from my life-long obsession with travel. It didn't take me long to discover the magic of Asian sauces, spice pastes and fresh aromatic herbs. These star ingredients galvanise your tastebuds with their salty, sour and pungent tastes. Practically anything can be made wondrous with them and, best of all, they aren't fattening.

Meals in Heels, my previous title with Murdoch Books, was all about make-ahead cooking for entertaining, *Skinny* is for the rest of the week. Time is of the essence in everyone's world, so most of these 130+ recipes can be made in 30 minutes or under one hour. Quick, delicious and healthy is the new cooking mantra for today's busy lives.

So cook your friends or family a guilt-free glamorous meal, and don't forget a glass of wine. It doesn't matter if you're wearing heels or slippers.

Jennifer Joyce

Skinny Tips

DON'T DIET, DON'T DENY YOURSELF…
JUST THINK SKINNY

It's been proven that exercise alone won't make you lose weight — it's all about what you eat. You don't have to count the calories or the fat, just use your common sense and judiciously cut back the fat. I still enjoy fried food, a creamy dessert or joint of meat on the weekend, but not every day. Making skinny, delicious food mid-week will vastly improve your diet and it doesn't mean missing out on flavour or a satisfying quantity. Here are some practical guidelines to smarter eating.

DON'T EAT BETWEEN MEALS
Snacking is one of the biggest reasons for weight gain. It keeps you from gauging whether you're hungry, full or just bored. If you change one thing … THIS IS IT! Eat three meals that include protein of some sort and you won't need to snack. It also gives your body a chance to burn off the calories you've eaten already. When the next meal rolls around, you'll most certainly be hungry. Food always tastes better when you're starving. Making sure you have protein in every meal is vital to making this work, otherwise you may feel tortured.

QUIT WHEN YOU'RE FULL
There isn't a law that says you have to finish your plate. Forget what your mother said when your stomach says 'full'. STOP! Overeating stretches your stomach and will increase your appetite. It's important to know when you're hungry or full,

and overeating confuses your stomach and brain. Later on, lethargy and nausea come into play, but then it's too late. Likewise, if you don't feel hungry at breakfast, don't feel that you have to eat. Wait until later in the morning and then eat. Your body will tell you when it's ready.

DON'T DENY YOURSELF THE GOOD TASTES
We all love the taste of bacon, feta cheese or a dollop of cream in food, and there is no reason why you should stop — just use far less. Instead of eight slices of bacon in a stew, use two. You will get all the smoky taste but not as much saturated fat. Same goes for cheese; instead of using half a block of parmesan or feta, just use a couple of tablespoons sprinkled over. It's vital in recipes to include a bit of these flavours, otherwise healthy cooking becomes a bit earnest and dull.

WINE AND COFFEE
You will be glad to know these favourites can help you — within reason of course. Both suppress your appetite, so if you're making dinner and want to devour a large slice of bread with butter, have a glass of wine instead. (Just don't drink the whole bottle before you tuck in.) Likewise, if you can't wait for lunch, drink a cup of coffee or tea. It will stave off hunger pains.

GOOD FAT VERSUS BAD FAT
There are two types of fat, saturated and unsaturated. Animal fat is the former and that's the area you want to considerably cut back on. Butter, cream, bacon and sausages are all in that list so keep them to a minimum if you can. Mono-unsaturated and poly-unsaturated fats are the virtuous types, and these include:

olive oil, vegetable oils, nuts, olives and avocado. Although
still high in calories, they won't give you cholesterol. Your
body still needs fat to maintain a nutritional balance, so keep
cooking with these.

VEGETABLES AND FRUIT
Nutritionists say you should eat five handfuls of fruit or veg a day
and the brighter the colour the better. It's not always possible,
and I certainly don't keep count. But consider throwing some
spinach, green beans or other quick-cooking vegetable into your
main dish if it works. It saves washing another pot and you get
a bit more health into your diet. Eating raw vegetables is also
important, so toss a little side salad together or eat a raw carrot
while cooking. The extra fibre keeps your gut clean and helps
wipe out toxins left in the body.

VARY WHAT YOU EAT
Eat a wide variety of foods so that you can take in all the
nutrients your body needs. Make a grainy salad every couple
of weeks, boil lentils instead of rice, go vegetarian a few nights
or try tofu. Avoid cooking the same things over and over, such as
pasta or steak. It's good to have red meat one night, but not three
times a week. Avoid too many sandwiches for lunch, and vary
it with main-sized salads or hearty soups. Cooking seasonally
also encourages you to cook a variety of vegetables, fish and
fruit. It costs much less and is more environmentally friendly
than using non-seasonal foods.

FOLLOW THE EXAMPLE OF THE FRENCH AND ITALIAN

If you eat something rich at home or in a restaurant, then make sure you eat vegetables or salad with it. Although the Italians and French indulge in fried foods, rich meats and creamy cheese as part of their wonderful cuisines, they also consume a vast array of vegetables and fruit. Salad is eaten after nearly all meals. Overweight people are rarely seen in these countries due to their common-sense eating, legume-rich diet, minimal snacking and love of seasonal vegetables.

USE YOUR FREEZER MORE

We all have nights when we lose the will to cook. Sometimes it's too late, you're tired and take-away is just a phone call away. The next time you cook something healthy, make double and freeze the other portion. If you marinate meat or poultry for grilling, freeze a few extra pieces with the sauce. When it thaws, it will soak up all the lovely flavours and will be ready to barbecue. Freeze leftover rice in zip-lock bags and use it for fried rice.

STOCK UP YOUR KITCHEN WITH GOOD FOOD

If you want to eat well, a little shopping and planning is required. Stock up your cupboard and freezer with core basics to cook with and your weekly shop won't be so arduous. Have a decent selection of spices, Asian ingredients, vinegars and oils so that you don't have to scramble mid-week to find them. Make a big grocery trip once a week with a few dinners planned and buy some fresh vegetables to use ad hoc. For the nights you're not organised, use the cupboard to pull from and whip up risottos, chicken dishes, stir-fries with noodles, or a big main-course salad.

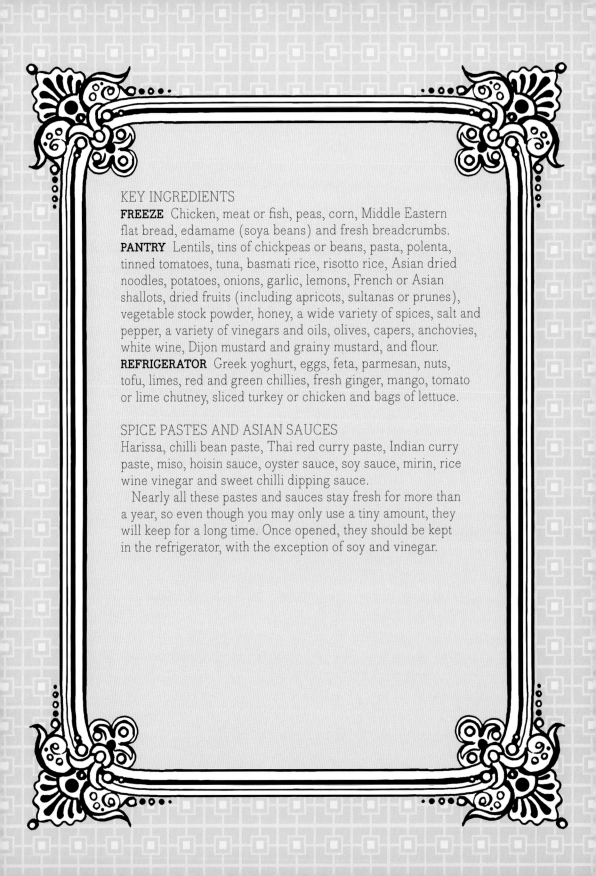

KEY INGREDIENTS
FREEZE Chicken, meat or fish, peas, corn, Middle Eastern flat bread, edamame (soya beans) and fresh breadcrumbs.
PANTRY Lentils, tins of chickpeas or beans, pasta, polenta, tinned tomatoes, tuna, basmati rice, risotto rice, Asian dried noodles, potatoes, onions, garlic, lemons, French or Asian shallots, dried fruits (including apricots, sultanas or prunes), vegetable stock powder, honey, a wide variety of spices, salt and pepper, a variety of vinegars and oils, olives, capers, anchovies, white wine, Dijon mustard and grainy mustard, and flour.
REFRIGERATOR Greek yoghurt, eggs, feta, parmesan, nuts, tofu, limes, red and green chillies, fresh ginger, mango, tomato or lime chutney, sliced turkey or chicken and bags of lettuce.

SPICE PASTES AND ASIAN SAUCES
Harissa, chilli bean paste, Thai red curry paste, Indian curry paste, miso, hoisin sauce, oyster sauce, soy sauce, mirin, rice wine vinegar and sweet chilli dipping sauce.

Nearly all these pastes and sauces stay fresh for more than a year, so even though you may only use a tiny amount, they will keep for a long time. Once opened, they should be kept in the refrigerator, with the exception of soy and vinegar.

KITCHEN EQUIPMENT

There are certain items that can help you cook with less fat.
The most important is a good-quality non-stick frying pan.
Buy a brand with a thick heavy base that distributes heat
evenly while cooking.

Next is a large heavy-based saucepan. If you cook onions
slowly in them, then not as much oil is required.

Other useful items include: pastry brush for brushing oil, spray
oil mister, cast-iron chargrill (griddle) pan, glass jam jars for
making vinaigrettes, citrus zester, electric spice grinder, mortar
and pestle, large shallow baking dishes, large baking trays,
wire mesh sieve and, of course, a good sharp chopping knife.

Snacks & Nibbles

Oven-dried cherry tomatoes with lemon-oregano salt

preparation time 10 minutes / **cooking time** 1½ hours / **makes** 2 cups

Oven drying has been an epiphany for me while writing this book. The flavours of oven-dried vegetables and fruit intensify for a powerful taste. Lemon and oregano salt makes these cherry tomatoes taste like heaven. Unlike most dehydrating, you don't need to dry these overnight, only 1½ hours on very low heat.

400 g (14 oz) baby roma (plum) tomatoes
finely grated zest of 1 lemon
2 teaspoons dried wild oregano
2 garlic cloves, thinly sliced
1 teaspoon sea salt

Preheat the oven to 100°C (200°F/Gas ½). Halve the tomatoes and place, cut side up, on a baking tray. Mix together the lemon zest, oregano, garlic and salt. Sprinkle over the tomato. Place in the oven for 1½ hours or until semi-dried. They are ready to eat or add to salads.

PREP AHEAD

These will keep for 1 week in the refrigerator in an airtight container.

THE SKINNY

There is absolutely no oil used, which means no fat. Tomatoes are packed with lycopene, an antioxidant that wards off disease.

Little pickled vegetables

preparation time 15 minutes / cooking time 5 minutes / pickling time 28 hours / makes 4 cups

There is nothing like a crunchy pickled vegetable with a hint of sweetness and the tang of vinegar. I have tried many variations of pickles and the key to a crisp texture is salting the vegetables beforehand. You don't need to properly can (bottle) these because they won't last that long. Just pour them into a glass or plastic container and refrigerate for 24 hours.

3 zucchini (courgettes), cut into 1 cm (½ inch) thick slices
2 long red capsicums (peppers), such as romero, cut into slices, or 6 sweet baby capsicums cut into fat rings
1 telegraph (long) cucumber, seeds removed and cut into chunks
1 brown onion, thickly sliced
4 tablespoons sea salt

Pickling liquid
500 ml (17 fl oz/2 cups) cider vinegar
150 g (5½ oz/1⅔ cup) caster (superfine) sugar
2 tablespoons yellow mustard seeds
1 large pinch of chilli flakes

Mix all the vegetables with the salt, place in a sieve over a bowl and leave for 4 hours or overnight in the refrigerator.

Rinse them well afterwards and place in a 1 litre (35 fl oz/4 cup) capacity glass jar with a lid.

To make the pickling liquid, place all the ingredients in a saucepan over medium heat and bring to the boil. Cook for 5 minutes until slightly syrupy. Pour over the vegetables, cool, then cover and refrigerate. Leave to pickle for at least 24 hours.

PREP AHEAD

These will keep for 1 week in the refrigerator in an airtight container.

THE SKINNY

Pickles of any sort make a healthy low-calorie snack. If using store-bought versions, then be sure they aren't too high in salt.

Spicy pumpkin and sunflower seeds

preparation time 5 minutes / cooking time 15 minutes / makes 1¼ cups

If you want a quick nibble that's healthy and tasty, these spicy salted seeds will satisfy your peckish cravings. Use to sprinkle on salads as well.

150 g (5½ oz/1 cup) pepitas
   (pumpkin seeds)
3 tablespoons sunflower seeds
1 tablespoon olive oil
1 teaspoon smoked paprika
1 teaspoon caster (superfine) sugar
1 teaspoon sea salt

Preheat the oven to 180°C (350°F/Gas 4). Mix all the ingredients together in a bowl and spread in a single layer on a baking tray. Bake for 10–15 minutes or until golden at the edges. Remove and cool.

PREP AHEAD

These will keep for 2 weeks in an airtight container.

THE SKINNY

High in fibre and health, these make a spicy nibble to have with a drink — much better than crisps.

Oven-dried root vegetable crisps

preparation time 15 minutes / cooking time 1¼ hours / makes 2 cups

I know it sounds ridiculous to make your own crisps but these will have you hooked. Forget that these are skinny snacks — the concentrated taste of the vegetables with a sprinkle of sea salt is glorious. I tried many cooking methods when making these and low heat works best. If baked at higher temperatures, they don't cook evenly and burn at the edges. Making your own is easy, but it's advisable to pick up a mandolin to slice them; the cheap plastic versions work fine and stay sharp for a long time.

2 beetroot (beets), scrubbed and
   unpeeled
2 parsnips, scrubbed and unpeeled
1 sweet potato (kumara), scrubbed
   and unpeeled
1½ tablespoons vegetable oil, for oiling

Preheat the oven to 110°C (225°F/Gas ½). Using a mandolin, slice the vegetables to about 3 mm (⅛ inch) thick. Place on oiled baking trays in a single layer and sprinkle with sea salt. Cook for 1¼ hours or until the slices start to curl up around the edges. As all ovens differ slightly, keep an eye on the crisps during the last 10 minutes of cooking. Even if they are slightly chewy in the centre, when you remove them, they will crisp up on cooling. Remove from the oven, cool, then store immediately in an airtight container.

PREP AHEAD

Store in an airtight container for 2–3 days.

THE SKINNY

Oven drying is a useful way to crisp up fruits and vegetables. Store-bought versions can be very expensive and potentially full of fat and sugar. These are an ideal skinny snack to replace crisps and other junk food.

Turkish pepper and feta salsa with pita crisps

preparation time 20 minutes / cooking time 10 minutes / makes 2 cups

This finely diced Middle Eastern salsa incorporates all the sweet, sour and salty tastes we crave. Scoop up bites with crisp baked pita triangles for a guilt-free treat. I like to use the long pointy romero capsicums but you can also use bell or gypsy. The key is to cut everything up nice and tiny so it picks up the other flavours.

Turkish pepper and feta salsa

2 tablespoons pomegranate molasses
1 tablespoon tomato paste
  (concentrated purée)
1 small red capsicum (pepper),
  finely diced
1 small cucumber, seeds removed
  and finely diced
1 small red onion, finely diced
2 tablespoons finely chopped mint
2 tablespoons crumbled feta cheese

Pita crisps

6 pita breads
olive oil spray
1 tablespoon sumac or mild chilli
  powder (optional)

To make the pita crisps, preheat the oven to 200°C (400°F/Gas 6). Using a pair of scissors, cut around the edges of the pita bread and remove. Cut the remaining part into large triangles and pull apart. Place on a baking tray and spray with the olive oil. Sprinkle with sea salt, freshly ground black pepper and sumac or chilli powder. Bake for 8–10 minutes or until golden. Remove and cool.

Meanwhile, make the salsa. Mix the pomegranate molasses and tomato paste in a bowl and season. Mix in the remaining ingredients. Serve with the pita crisps.

PREP AHEAD

The pita crisps can be stored for 3 days in an airtight container. The salsa can be covered and refrigerated for 1 day.

THE SKINNY

Baked pita crisps have little oil and far fewer calories than crisps or tortilla chips, making them a much healthier option. Olive oil sprays are a great buy because it means you don't need to use much oil when cooking.

Padrón peppers with honey and paprika

preparation time 5 minutes / cooking time 5 minutes / serves 4

You can buy Padrón peppers at supermarkets, delis or Spanish food stores. They are tiny green peppers with a mild taste but, be warned, there is always one spicy one per bag. Flash-fry them in a hot frying pan and serve straight up. Hold them by their stem to bite off the warm pepper.

1 tablespoon olive oil
200 g (7 oz) Padrón peppers
1 tablespoon honey
1 teaspoon sherry vinegar
½ teaspoon smoked paprika

Heat the oil in a frying pan until nearly smoking hot. Add the peppers and allow to sizzle for 3 or so minutes. They will puff up and brown, so toss them around in the pan a bit so they don't burn. Transfer to a platter.

Mix the honey and vinegar together and drizzle over the peppers. Sprinkle with the paprika and season with sea salt.

PREP AHEAD

The peppers should be cooked just before serving.

THE SKINNY

Padrón and other pan-fried peppers are full of health and make a quick skinny bite.

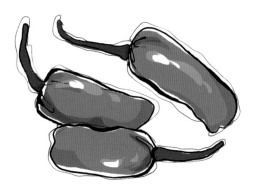

Tarragon-marinated baby mushrooms

preparation time 5 minutes / marinating time 30 minutes / makes 2 cups

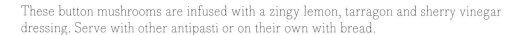

These button mushrooms are infused with a zingy lemon, tarragon and sherry vinegar dressing. Serve with other antipasti or on their own with bread.

200 g (7 oz) small button mushrooms, trimmed
1 garlic clove
juice of ½ lemon
1 tablespoon chopped tarragon
1 tablespoon Champagne or good-quality white wine vinegar
1 tablespoon extra virgin olive oil

Toss all the ingredients together in a bowl. Leave to marinate at room temperature for 30 minutes.

Just before serving, toss a couple of times to coat everything. Remove the garlic clove and serve with little toothpicks.

PREP AHEAD

The mushrooms can be made 1 day ahead, covered and refrigerated.

THE SKINNY

Marinated mushrooms are healthy nibbles that are skimpy on calories.

Marinated olives with fennel, lemon and celery

preparation time 10 minutes / makes 1½ cups

My mother used to buy a mix of this sort from our Italian deli and I loved picking out the tangy onions and celery. Oil-cured olives are preferable over Kalamata or other brined varieties as they have less salt and a milder flavour.

175 g (6 oz/1 cup) oil-cured
　　black olives
2 celery stalks, from the heart,
　　thinly sliced
½ small red onion, chopped
1 tablespoon finely grated lemon zest
1 tablespoon extra virgin olive oil
1 tablespoon red wine vinegar
1 teaspoon fennel seeds

Mix all the ingredients together in a small bowl and serve.

PREP AHEAD

These will keep for 1 week in the refrigerator in an airtight container.

THE SKINNY

Yes, olives are high in fat, but 'fat' doesn't always mean fattening. Olives have the good kind of fat, mono-unsaturated, which is beneficial for your heart. You're not going to eat this whole portion yourself — it's meant to be a little bite to have with drinks.

Spiced garlic flat bread

preparation time 5 minutes / cooking time 10 minutes / makes 16

If you're serving up a Middle Eastern meal, this fragrant bread can be made in less than 10 minutes. The round khobez bread is usually sold near the pita bread at the supermarket.

1 tablespoon olive oil
2 round Middle Eastern flat breads (khobez) or Lebanese breads
1 garlic clove, finely chopped
1 tablespoon za'atar or Berber Middle Eastern spice mix
2 tablespoons flat-leaf (Italian) parsley, finely chopped

Preheat the oven to 200°C (400°F/Gas 6). Brush the olive oil over the flat breads and scatter with the garlic, spices and some sea salt and freshly ground black pepper. Place on a baking tray and cook for 7–8 minutes or until crisp at the edges. Scatter over the parsley and cut into triangles.

PREP AHEAD

The flat bread can be prepared, unbaked, on the morning of serving and heated just before you're ready to eat.

THE SKINNY

Spice mixes are indispensable for making quick mezze. Along with the garlic, it elevates the flat bread into a warm intoxicating snack.

American-style prawn cocktail

preparation time 5 minutes / serves 4

Every country seems to have their own rendition of the prawn cocktail. Americans call it shrimp cocktail and make a dipping sauce spiked with horseradish and, dare I say, ketchup. There is no denying its retro allure. Say goodbye to bland rose marie sauce and hello to the American cousin's version.

150 ml (5 fl oz) tomato sauce (ketchup)
1 tablespoon freshly grated horseradish
   or store-bought horseradish cream
1 lemon, juiced to yield 1 teaspoon
   and the rest quartered
1 tablespoon finely chopped celery
1 teaspoon Worcestershire sauce
½ teaspoon Tabasco or hot pepper
   sauce
1–2 heads baby gem lettuce,
   leaves separated
300 g (10½ oz) cooked peeled
   large prawns (shrimp)

Mix together the tomato sauce, horseradish, lemon juice, celery and Worcestershire and Tabasco sauces in a small bowl and season with sea salt and freshly ground black pepper.

Arrange the lettuce on a platter or plate and top with the prawns. Serve the cocktail sauce alongside.

PREP AHEAD

All the components can be prepared 1 day ahead, refrigerated, then assembled the following day.

THE SKINNY

Prawns are full of protein to fill you up and have almost nil fat.

Crisp tofu bites with chilli soy-vinegar sauce

preparation time 10 minutes / cooking time 5 minutes / makes 32

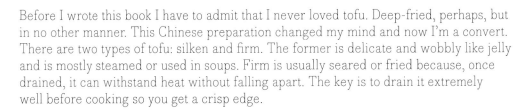

Before I wrote this book I have to admit that I never loved tofu. Deep-fried, perhaps, but in no other manner. This Chinese preparation changed my mind and now I'm a convert. There are two types of tofu: silken and firm. The former is delicate and wobbly like jelly and is mostly steamed or used in soups. Firm is usually seared or fried because, once drained, it can withstand heat without falling apart. The key is to drain it extremely well before cooking so you get a crisp edge.

1 x 350 g (12 oz) packet firm tofu
1 tablespoon sesame seeds
1 tablespoon sesame oil
1 red bird's eye chilli, seeds removed
   and finely chopped
1 tablespoon soy sauce
1 tablespoon Chinese black
   or red wine vinegar
1 teaspoon caster (superfine) sugar
2 spring onions (scallions),
   finely chopped

Wrap the tofu with lots of paper towel. Press firmly to remove all the excess water. You may need to do this a couple of times to get all the water out. Halve the tofu lengthways, then cut each piece into 16 cubes. Toss with the sesame seeds.

Heat the sesame oil in a non-stick frying pan until very hot. Add the tofu and brown at least 2–3 sides, about 1 minute each side. Use 2 teaspoons or a pair of chopsticks to turn them over when browned. Drain on paper towel.

Combine the chilli, soy sauce, vinegar and sugar in a bowl. Arrange the tofu on a platter. Spoon the sauce over and scatter with the spring onion. Serve immediately.

PREP AHEAD

You can wrap the tofu in paper towel and leave to drain all day in the refrigerator, and the sauce can be made on the morning of serving. Fry just before serving.

THE SKINNY

Tofu is full of health and the skinny soy-vinegar sauce gives it the taste it needs.

Instant skinny snacks

We all get that moment in our day when we feel insanely famished but can't be bothered to make anything. Two hours after lunch or just before dinner are the desperate hours when your blood sugar drops and crisps, cheese and other junk food beckons. Whether it's just grazing or arranging a little platter of tidbits for friends and family, this list is a useful reminder of the 'good' snacks to have on hand when you're peckish. Most of these items keep for a long time in the fridge or cupboard so stock up on your favorites for those critical hungry moments.

SNACKS FOR GRAZING, ON THE GO OR AT THE OFFICE
- dried apricots, cherries or raisins
- raw nuts
- wasabi peas
- steamed edamame (soya beans) with salt
- sliced apples and pears
- rice crackers
- vegetable crudité
- popcorn
- low-fat crackers, such as Ryvita
- plain bagel crisps
- baked pita chips
- baked tortilla chips with fresh salsa
- pretzels with honey-mustard dip
- soy-roasted sunflower seeds or pepitas (pumpkin seeds) or a mix
- pickled cucumber

MIDDLE EASTERN NIBBLES
- low-fat hummus
- baba ghanoush
- low-fat Greek yoghurt (mixed with a little harissa or other spice)
- dukkah-spice dip with crudité and hard-boiled eggs
- warm flat bread
- crisp baby romaine lettuce leaves
- fresh radishes and cucumbers
- pistachios in the shell
- olives
- jarred roasted peppers, mixed with harissa or chilli and oil

ANTIPASTI OR TAPAS
- marinated olives
- caperberries
- tinned lupuni beans
- dried broad (fava) beans
- sun-blushed or sun-dried tomatoes
- jarred marinated artichoke hearts
- grissini (breadsticks)
- marinated fresh anchovy fillets
- toasted almonds or other nuts
- pickled vegetables
- peperoncini (Italian pickled peppers) or peppadews (pickled red cherry peppers)
- pickled garlic
- toasted sourdough bread rubbed with olive oil and a garlic clove
- melon or purple figs with prosciutto (Parma ham) or jamón (serrano ham)
- low-fat tzatziki dip

SCANDINAVIAN FISH AND BREAD
- smoked mackerel or trout fillets
- gravadlax or smoked salmon
- small cooked prawns or tinned crabmeat
- toasted brown, pumpernickel or rye bread
- sliced red onions
- capers
- freshly grated horseradish or prepared horseradish cream
- sliced cucumber
- sweet or Dijon mustard
- quartered cherry tomatoes
- sliced pickled beetroot
- fresh dill or spring onions (scallions)

Starters

Sashimi tuna with yuzu dressing

preparation time 5 minutes / freezing time 10 minutes / serves 4

If you have access to outstanding fresh fish, sashimi isn't as intimidating as one would imagine. If using tuna, choose a good-quality, deep red piece with as little marbling as possible. A sharp knife and freezing the fish for 10 minutes before preparing makes slicing very easy. Yuzu juice is a Japanese citrus juice, which is available in bottles from Japanese grocers. It tastes like a cross between grapefruit and lime and can be easily substituted with just that.

300 g (10½ oz) piece of ruby-red tuna
   or sea bass, skin removed
2 spring onions (scallions), finely
   chopped
4 handfuls mizuna, or 1 punnet
   baby mustard leaves
2 tablespoons chopped chives

Yuzu dressing
½ garlic clove
3 tablespoons yuzu juice (or equal
   parts grapefruit and lime juice)
1 teaspoon soy sauce
1 teaspoon peanut oil

Place the fish in the freezer for 10 minutes to firm up, then slice as thin as possible with a very sharp knife.

Meanwhile, make the yuzu dressing. Pound the garlic clove using a mortar and pestle to a paste or use the flat edge of a knife. Mix in the remaining dressing ingredients and crack some black pepper in.

Arrange the fish, spring onion and leaves on plates and pour over the dressing. Sprinkle with the chives.

PREP AHEAD

The fish can be sliced 4 hours ahead and stored between sheets of baking paper in the fridge; plastic wrap isn't ideal as it makes the fish sweat.

THE SKINNY

Sashimi is about as healthy and easy as food gets. The yuzu-soy dressing has a scant amount of oil and makes a great salty-sour dipping sauce.

Tomato tartines with goat's cheese and caper, mint and balsamic dressing

preparation time 20 minutes / **cooking time** 5 minutes / **serves** 4

Tartine is a gorgeous French term for an open-faced sandwich. Alongside some salad, it makes an elegant starter or lunch. Make this when tomatoes are in their summer glory and choice varieties abound.

4 thick slices sourdough bread
1 garlic clove
250 g (9 oz) mixed tomatoes, such as cherry, yellow, zebra, marmara, green or roma (plum)
50 g (1¾ oz) soft goat's cheese
2 small French shallots (eschalots), thinly sliced

Caper, mint and balsamic dressing

3 tablespoons finely chopped mint
3 tablespoons extra virgin olive oil
2 tablespoons balsamic vinegar
1 tablespoon capers in brine, drained and chopped
2 teaspoons caster (superfine) sugar

To make the caper, mint and balsamic dressing, place all the ingredients in a small glass jar with a lid, season with sea salt and freshly ground black pepper and shake well.

Trim the bread into large squares or rectangles and toast. Rub with the garlic clove and season with salt and pepper. Slice the tomatoes into quarters or halves depending on their size. Spread the goat's cheese on the toast, top with the tomato and pour the dressing over. Top with the shallot and serve.

PREP AHEAD

The dressing can be made 8 hours ahead, but assemble the tomato, cheese and bread just before eating.

THE SKINNY

Tartines make a great replacement for pastry but you still get the crunch factor. The amount of goat's cheese used here is only minimal but greatly contributes to the flavour.

Fresh beef and mango spring rolls

preparation time 1 hour / **cooking time** 10 minutes / **makes** 8

On a magical trip to Vietnam, I ate this surprising combination. The Vietnamese are the masters of fresh delicate food that utilises healthy ingredients. Fruit and meat in fresh spring rolls was not a pairing I had tasted before, but the sweet mango complemented the rich beef. Pineapple and sliced cooked pork was another pairing that I tasted and it was equally good.

olive oil spray

250 g (9 oz) piece of beef fillet,
　trimmed of all fat

8 round rice paper wrappers
　(15 cm/6 inches in diameter),
　plus extra to have as spares

1 mango, cut into 1 cm (½ inch)
　thick pieces

2 red Asian shallots, thinly sliced

1 small handful mint leaves

1 small handful basil leaves

8 coriander (cilantro) sprigs,
　about 7.5 cm (3 inches) long

1 bunch chives

Dipping sauce

4 tablespoons lime juice

2 tablespoons fish sauce

2 tablespoons water

1 thumb-sized red chilli, halved,
　seeds removed and thinly sliced

1 garlic clove, finely chopped

Heat a non-stick frying pan over high heat, spray with oil and season the beef with sea salt and freshly ground black pepper. Sear the meat for 2–3 minutes each side. Allow to rest for 10 minutes. Thinly slice and set aside.

Meanwhile, make the dipping sauce, mix all the ingredients together and pour into a couple of small bowls.

Place a large tea towel on a work surface. Fill a wide shallow bowl with warm water. Soak a rice paper wrapper in the water for about 30 seconds. When soft and pliable, place the wrapper on the tea towel and wipe off the excess water with another towel. Place a small pile of beef, mango, shallot, mint, basil and coriander at the bottom of the wrapper. Fold the sides in, then roll up tightly to enclose. Just before you finish rolling it up all the way, place a chive in the spring roll and finish rolling up. Place, seam side down, on another tea towel. Repeat with the remaining wrappers and filling.

Throw away any wrappers that rip and start
again with a fresh one. It may take a few tries
to get the knack so don't get discouraged. If
the wrapper is too soft, it will fall apart, and if
it's too hard, it will not stick together. Practise
soaking a few so you can get a feel for the right
consistency.

When ready to serve, cut each spring roll
in half diagonally with a very sharp knife.
Serve with the dipping sauce.

PREP AHEAD

Spring rolls can be made 12 hours
ahead. Store on a tray lined with baking
paper, cover with more baking paper,
then plastic wrap. This keeps them
from drying out. Refrigerate until
ready to serve.

THE SKINNY

Fresh Vietnamese spring rolls don't contain
any oil and can be filled with all sorts of
ingredients from rice noodles to chicken
or prawns. They are a tasty guilt-free treat.

Steamed asparagus with chopped egg vinaigrette

preparation time 10 minutes / cooking time 5 minutes / serves 4

Spring is asparagus's time to shine, and this ravishing sauce brings out the best in the knobbly green spears. It's based on the French ravigote dressing, which sometimes has tarragon and mustard as well.

16 thick asparagus spears, trimmed

Chopped egg vinaigrette
2 tablespoons extra virgin olive oil
1½ tablespoons red wine vinegar
1 tablespoon finely chopped flat-leaf (Italian) parsley
1 teaspoon capers in brine, drained and finely chopped
1 French shallot (eschalot), finely diced
1 hard-boiled egg, finely chopped

To make the chopped egg vinaigrette, mix all the ingredients in a small bowl with some sea salt and freshly ground black pepper. Whisk until smooth and set aside.

Steam the asparagus for 3 minutes or blanch for 2 minutes in salted boiling water. Drain and serve warm with the vinaigrette drizzled over.

PREP AHEAD

The asparagus can be blanched and rinsed in cold water 6 hours ahead and refrigerated. Warm again by submerging in boiling water for 30 seconds. The vinaigrette should be prepared only 2 hours ahead to keep the herbs green.

THE SKINNY

Steamed vegetables are a no-brainer for skinny food. A chunky vinaigrette uses less oil than mayonnaise or a cream-based sauce.

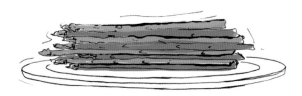

Beef carpaccio with rocket, spring onion and parmesan shavings

preparation time 20 minutes / freezing time 30 minutes / serves 4

This classic Italian starter is easy to slice if you partially freeze the meat before cutting. Chopped radicchio leaves are also good scattered over.

400 g (14 oz) piece of beef fillet, trimmed of all fat
3 tablespoons extra virgin olive oil
2 tablespoons finely chopped spring onion (scallion)
4 handfuls rocket (arugula) leaves
2 tablespoons good-quality aged balsamic vinegar
2 tablespoons parmesan shavings
1 lemon, cut into wedges

Heat a non-stick frying pan over medium–high heat until very hot. Rub the beef with a tiny amount of the olive oil and season well with sea salt and freshly ground black pepper. Sear quickly for 1 minute each side until just browned all over. Remove, cool, then wrap in plastic wrap and place in the freezer for 30 minutes or until firm but not frozen.

Using a very sharp knife, slice the meat into 5 mm (¼ inch) thick pieces or as thin as you can. You will need 3–4 slices per serving, depending on the size of the fillet. When the fillet gets too small to slice, just pound out the remaining pieces between two sheets of baking paper and slice into similar sized pieces. Arrange the slices in a single layer on plates. Season, scatter over the spring onion and place a handful of rocket on top of each. Drizzle with the vinegar and remaining olive oil. Scatter over the parmesan shavings and serve with a lemon wedge.

PREP AHEAD

You can slice the meat 4 hours ahead, drizzle it with olive oil and refrigerate it, covered in plastic wrap. Just be sure to wrap the beef tightly to keep it from discolouring.

THE SKINNY

Carpaccio is not only delicious but also very low in fat, uses very little oil and is high in protein. You're guaranteed to be happy and full.

Vegetable and spring onion pancakes with dipping sauce

preparation time 10 minutes / cooking time 25 minutes / serves 4

These Korean-inspired pancakes are fast to whip up and don't require much oil to cook them. Serve up with a spicy green salad and use the dipping sauce to dress it.

100 g (3½ oz/⅔ cup) self-raising flour
75 ml (2⅓ fl oz) low-fat milk
3 eggs, lightly beaten
180 g (6⅓ oz/2 cups) bean sprouts
6 spring onions (scallions),
    cut into 3 cm (1¼ inch) lengths
450 g (1 lb) sweet potato (kumara)
    (about 1), peeled and cut into
    thin matchsticks
vegetable oil spray

Chilli-soy dipping sauce
3 tablespoons rice vinegar
2 tablespoons soy sauce
1 tablespoon sesame seeds, toasted
1 red bird's eye chilli, sliced
1 tablespoon caster (superfine) sugar

To make the chilli-soy dipping sauce, combine all the ingredients in a bowl, stir and set aside.

Place the flour and a pinch of sea salt and freshly ground black pepper in a large bowl. While whisking continuously, add the milk and egg. Whisk until a smooth batter forms, then add the bean sprouts, spring onion and sweet potato and gently combine. The mixture should be thick.

Heat a large non-stick frying pan over medium–low heat and spray with a tiny bit of oil. Spoon one-quarter cupfuls of batter into the pan to make 3–4 pancakes at a time and cook for about 4 minutes each side, making sure the sweet potato is cooked. Serve with the sauce. Makes 8 pancakes.

PREP AHEAD

The vegetables can be chopped ahead and stored in a bowl of cold water. Drain and dry before mixing with the flour and eggs. Make the batter up to 1 hour ahead. The dipping sauce can be prepared 8 hours ahead.

THE SKINNY

Vegetable pancakes don't have to be caloric if you use a heavy non-stick pan and oil spray, and with long, low heat you can achieve a crisp exterior.

Miso vegetable yakitori

preparation time 20 minutes / cooking time 5 minutes / serves 4

One of my favourite Japanese restaurants in London is Tosa. It's a proper yakitoria with a charcoal grill. One of their signature dishes is the onion lollipops. These are easy to make, along with the other two types of skewers here. Eat as a snack or with rice.

1 red onion
4 fat spring onions (scallions)
1 small eggplant (aubergine)
8 shiitake mushrooms
2 tablespoons vegetable oil or oil spray

Miso glaze
2 tablespoons white miso paste
2 tablespoons mirin
1 tablespoon caster (superfine) sugar

If using wooden skewers, remember to soak them in water for 10 minutes before using. Cut the onion into 4 thick slices. Slice the white part of the spring onions into 4 cm (1½ inch) chunks and finely chop the green part to garnish later. Cut the eggplant into 2.5 cm (1 inch) chunks.

To make the miso glaze, mix all the ingredients in a bowl and set aside.

Thread 2 mushrooms onto a skewer, with a spring onion chunk in between to make 4 skewers. For the onion lollipops, run a skewer through each slice. For the eggplant skewers, thread about 3–4 chunks onto 4 skewers each. Brush or spray all the vegetables with the oil and season with sea salt and freshly ground black pepper.

Preheat a barbecue or chargrill (griddle) pan to high. Grill the skewers for 2 minutes each side, then brush with the miso glaze. Scatter over the reserved chopped spring onion.

PREP AHEAD

The skewers and miso glaze can be made 8 hours ahead and refrigerated. Grill just before serving.

THE SKINNY

Miso makes a tasty glaze for barbecuing vegetables, fish, poultry or meat. Made from fermented soya beans, it is packed with health and only has a few calories.

Steamed globe artichokes with lemon and oregano dipping sauce

preparation time 15 minutes / cooking time 30 minutes / serves 4

If you have a steamer or pasta pot with a fitted insert, it's perfect for this. You want the large artichokes to steam rather than sit in the water and become soggy. When they're done, dip the leaves in the sauce, then zip the leaves through your front teeth to eat. When you get to the heart (the good bit), remember to discard the fuzzy choke with a spoon. This can be removed beforehand, but it's a bit of an arduous task.

4 globe artichokes
1 lemon, halved

Lemon-oregano dipping sauce
3 tablespoons extra virgin olive oil
1 tablespoon chopped oregano
   or 1 teaspoon dried wild oregano
1 garlic clove, bruised
1 French shallot (eschalot),
   finely chopped
finely grated zest and juice of 1 lemon
1 large pinch of chilli flakes

Place 2–3 sturdy and heatproof mugs upside-down in the base of a large stockpot. Pour in 7.5 cm (3 inches) water and bring to the boil. Remove the stems from the artichokes and pull off the very hard leaves at the base. Using scissors, cut the tips off all the leaves. Squeeze one half of the lemon over them. Place the artichokes, right side up, on top of the mugs, so that they will steam rather than sit in the water. Squeeze in the remaining lemon half, cover with the lid and steam for 30 minutes or until a skewer inserted into the thickest part of the artichokes withdraws easily.

Meanwhile, make the lemon-oregano dipping sauce. Whisk all the ingredients in a small bowl with some sea salt and freshly ground black pepper. Leave it to sit with the garlic, so the flavour comes through.

Pour the dressing into 4 small bowls and serve with the steamed artichokes.

PREP AHEAD

Prepare the dipping sauce a couple of hours ahead and refrigerate. Trim the artichokes 4 hours ahead but keep in some water with lemon juice added to keep the edges from blackening.

THE SKINNY

This is an easy way to prepare globe artichokes. The steaming and vinaigrette dipping sauce keeps the calories and fat paltry. Apart from being delicious, they are fun to eat.

Crisp pork in lettuce cups with chilli-lime dressing

preparation time 15 minutes / cooking time 10 minutes / serves 4

This speedy starter, known as 'larb' in Thailand, is an impressive dish to throw together for a snack or appetiser. The pork is pan-fried until crisp, then tossed with a sweet and sour lime dressing.

2 lemongrass stalks
1 tablespoon vegetable oil
400 g (14 oz) lean minced
   (ground) pork
1 tablespoon grated palm sugar
   (jaggery) or soft brown sugar
1 small red onion, finely diced
1 handful coriander (cilantro) leaves,
   chopped, plus extra sprigs for serving
2 heads baby gem or cos (romaine)
   lettuce, leaves separated, washed
   and chilled

Chilli-lime dressing
4 tablespoons lime juice
1 tablespoon fish sauce
1 tablespoon grated palm sugar
   (jaggery) or soft brown sugar
1 garlic clove, finely chopped
1 thumb-sized red chilli, seeds removed
   and finely chopped

To make the chilli-lime dressing, mix all the ingredients together until the sugar has dissolved.

Remove the tough outer layers of the lemongrass until you get to the tender pale heart. Cut off and discard the green tops and trim 2–3 cm (¾–1¼ inches) off the base. Finely chop the remainder.

Heat the oil in a large wok over high heat. Add the pork and cook until crisp and brown on the bottom before breaking it up with a spoon. Add the lemongrass and cook for another 2–3 minutes or until tender. Add the sugar, stir again, then remove from the heat.

Pour the dressing over the warm pork and add the onion and coriander. Gently stir and serve with the chilled lettuce leaves for scooping up bits.

PREP AHEAD

The pork can be made 1 day ahead and refrigerated. Reheat and pour the dressing over just before serving.

THE SKINNY

Crisp baby gem or cos lettuce is a fresh and clean alternative to fried wrappers to use as a base for Thai or other Asian toppings. The chilli-lime dressing contains no oil and elevates the stir-fried pork.

Ceviche with rocket salad

preparation time 15 minutes / marinating time 1 hour / serves 6

Ceviche or raw fish sounds bizarre, but I urge you to give it a try. The trick is to slice the fish thin or in small pieces. Technically it's not raw because it cooks in the citrus juice. Once it turns pearly white, drain it, then re-dress it. My friend Victoria, an amazing food writer and caterer, gave me this light and captivating recipe.

300 g (10½ oz) lemon sole fillet
 (or other good-quality white fish),
 skin and bones removed
4 limes
1 French shallot (eschalot), finely
 chopped
1 tablespoon white wine vinegar
1 heaped teaspoon sea salt
1 tablespoon chopped coriander
 (cilantro)
1 teaspoon capers in brine, drained
 and rinsed
1 tablespoon extra virgin olive oil
1 thumb-sized red chilli, seeds removed
 and finely chopped
rocket (arugula) leaves, to serve

Slice the lemon sole into very small pieces and place in two separate bowls. Finely grate the zest of one lime, then juice it along with the other 2 limes. Cut the remaining lime into wedges.

Whisk together the shallot, vinegar, lime zest and juice and the salt. Divide the dressing between the 2 fish, cover and refrigerate for 1 hour.

Drain the fish, season with sea salt and freshly ground black pepper and toss together with the coriander, capers, olive oil and chilli. Spoon the fish onto plates. Place some rocket over the fish and serve with the lime wedges.

PREP AHEAD

The fish can be sliced 8 hours ahead and refrigerated, stored between layers of baking paper but not marinated until 1 hour before serving, otherwise it gets tough.

THE SKINNY

With its citrus dressing, chilli and capers, ceviche is very low in fat and stratospherically high in flavour.

Baked sesame prawns with roasted chilli dipping sauce

preparation time 20 minutes / cooking time 5 minutes / serves 4

Over the years I have experimented, mostly unsuccessfully, with baking Asian starters instead of frying them. This eggwhite and sesame seed coating was a revelation because it creates a crisp exterior while sealing in the juicy prawns.

16 raw large prawns (shrimp), peeled and deveined with tails left on
2 eggwhites
4 tablespoons toasted white sesame seeds
cooking oil spray
thinly sliced spring onion (scallion), to serve

Sticky chilli dipping sauce
200 ml (7 fl oz) rice wine vinegar
100 g caster (superfine) sugar
2 tablespoons chilli flakes
1 red Asian shallot, thinly sliced

Preheat the oven to 200°C (400°F/Gas 6). To make the sticky chilli dipping sauce, heat the vinegar and sugar with a large pinch of salt in a saucepan over medium heat. Bring to the boil, then simmer for 5 minutes or until syrupy. Remove from the heat and add the chilli flakes. Set aside until cool, then add the shallot.

Butterfly the prawns. To do this, make a deep cut down the back so they lay nearly flat. Whisk the eggwhite until just foamy, then dip the prawns in the eggwhite, allowing the excess to drain off. Season with sea salt and freshly ground black pepper and roll in the sesame seeds. Place on a baking tray, spray with a bit of oil and bake for 5 minutes or until they turn opaque and start to curl a bit. Serve warm, garnished with the spring onion, with the dipping sauce on the side.

PREP AHEAD

The prawns can be coated 2 hours before cooking and refrigerated, stored between layers of baking paper, then wrapped in plastic wrap. The dipping sauce can be made 1 day ahead, but don't add the shallots until closer to serving.

THE SKINNY

The eggwhite and sesame coating seals in the prawns and crisps while it bakes. No deep-fryers in sight!

Stromboli salad with tomato, fresh anchovies and oregano

preparation time 10 minutes / cooking time 5 minutes / serves 4

I remember when my family and I rented a house in Palermo, Sicily, and spent a day visiting the nearby Aeolian Islands. They are best known for their tiny capers, grown in the arid volcanic soil, and locally fished anchovies. The snowy-white fillets are marinated in vinegar and served with only a splash of olive oil. Fortunately, they export them so we can experience the same pleasures back home. I usually drain them from the oil they're packed in and give them a gentle rinse before using.

1 cup sourdough bread cubes

2 tablespoons extra virgin olive oil

6 ripe tomatoes, such as small beefsteak (oxheart), roma (plum) or baby romas, cut into small chunks

16 fresh marinated anchovy fillets

1 tablespoon chopped oregano

2 small French shallots (eschalots), thinly sliced

1 tablespoon baby capers in brine, drained and rinsed

1 tablespoon red wine vinegar

Preheat the oven to 200°C (400°F/Gas 6). Toss the bread cubes with 1 tablespoon of the olive oil and some sea salt and freshly ground black pepper. Bake for 5–6 minutes or until golden. Remove and allow to cool.

Combine the tomato, anchovy fillets, croûtons, oregano, shallot and capers in a big bowl. Just before serving, drizzle the vinegar and remaining olive oil over and season. Mix well and serve.

PREP AHEAD

The croûtons can be prepared 1 day ahead and stored in an airtight container. Chop up all the ingredients a couple of hours ahead but don't toss together until serving.

THE SKINNY

Pungent oregano and a tangy splash of red wine vinegar add flavour while keeping the oil quantity low. Marinated anchovies are low in fat but high in protein, making the salad more substantial.

Spicy scallops with avocado and mango salsa

preparation time 15 minutes / cooking time 5 minutes / serves 4

Large prawns can be used here, so feel free to substitute. The trick to getting a good sear on scallops is to get the frying pan smoking hot. Heavy old-fashioned cast-iron frying pans are ideal but use the best one you have.

12 scallops, trimmed and cleaned
1 teaspoon olive oil
1 teaspoon mild chilli powder
  or smoked paprika
1 lime, cut into wedges

Avocado and mango salsa
1 ripe avocado, diced
1 mango, diced
1 small red onion, finely diced
2 tablespoons chopped coriander
  (cilantro)
finely grated zest and juice of 1 lime
2 teaspoons chipotle Tabasco sauce or
  ¼ teaspoon regular Tabasco sauce

To make the avocado and mango salsa, mix the ingredients in a small bowl. Season with sea salt and freshly ground black pepper and set aside.

Rub the scallops with the oil and chilli powder and season well.

When you're ready to eat, divide the salsa between four plates. Heat a heavy-based non-stick frying pan over high heat until very hot. Sear the scallops for about 1 minute each side; let them get crisp and brown before you turn them. You will need to sear them in two batches so that the pan is not overcrowded. Top each plate with the scallops and a lime wedge and serve immediately.

PREP AHEAD

The whole dish may be prepped ahead but no more than an hour before serving. Cover with plastic wrap close to the surface to prevent the avocado from browning.

THE SKINNY

Avocado is considered high in fat but it's the good one, mono-unsaturated. It pairs very well with scallops. The salsa enhances the taste and keeps the dish skinny.

Salads for Dinner or On The Side

Turkish burghul salad

preparation time 30 minutes / **serves** 4–6

A Turkish au pair in my neighbourhood gave me this recipe and it's one of my favourite salads. It keeps for up to four days refrigerated, making it handy for lunchboxes or as an impromptu healthy meal alongside a grilled piece of meat. Traditionally, a Turkish pepper paste is used in place of the tomato paste but it's not that easy to get hold of. If you have access to a Turkish food store, sample the chilli powders and pastes — it will open a new world for you.

400 g (14 oz/2¼ cups) fine burghul (bulgur)

500 ml (17 fl oz/2 cups) boiling water

12 spring onions (scallions), thinly sliced

4 roma (plum) tomatoes, seeds removed and diced

1 small cucumber, seeds removed and diced

juice of 4 limes

1 small handful flat-leaf (Italian) parsley, chopped

1 small handful mint leaves, chopped

4 tablespoons extra virgin olive oil

3 tablespoons tomato paste (concentrated purée)

1 tablespoon pomegranate molasses (optional)

1 teaspoon mild chilli powder, or to taste

2 teaspoons sea salt

Place the burghul in a large bowl and cover with the water. Allow to stand for 10 minutes, then fluff up with a fork. Add the remaining ingredients and stir together. Serve at room temperature or chilled.

PREP AHEAD

The entire salad can be made, covered and refrigerated for up to 4 days.

THE SKINNY

Burghul is much healthier than couscous because of its high fibre content; the wheat is cracked, rather than finely milled, and sweeps your gut clean. It creates a textural base for healthy salads. If making ahead, stir through the herbs just before serving.

Roasted eggplant with goat's cheese, crisp flat bread and mint-chilli dressing

preparation time 15 minutes / cooking time 25 minutes / serves 4

Toasty chunks of roasted eggplant are tossed in a minty balsamic vinaigrette with crisp flat bread, a sprinkle of goat's cheese and some spicy rocket. Middle East meets West in this luscious mix. Pomegranate seeds are also nice sprinkled over.

2 eggplants (aubergines)
1 tablespoon extra virgin olive oil
2 pieces Middle Eastern flat bread
  or pita bread
150 g (5½ oz) mixed red and yellow
  cherry tomatoes
4 large handfuls rocket (arugula)
2 French shallots (eschalots),
  thinly sliced
50 g (1¾ oz) hard goat's cheese,
  crumbled

Mint-chilli dressing
3 tablespoons balsamic vinegar
2 tablespoons extra virgin olive oil
1 large handful mint leaves,
  finely chopped
1 thumb-sized red chilli, seeds removed
  and finely chopped
1 French shallot (eschalot), finely diced

Preheat the oven to 200°C (400°F/Gas 6). Slice the eggplants into 3 cm (1¼ inch) chunks. Drizzle with the olive oil and season with sea salt and freshly ground black pepper. Arrange on a baking tray and roast for 25 minutes or until browned.

Rip the flat bread into pieces and place on a baking tray. Just as the eggplant is nearly ready, pop the flat bread into the oven and bake for 8 minutes, then remove and place in a bowl.

To make the mint-chilli dressing, mix all the ingredients together in a small bowl and season.

Toss about one-third of the dressing with the eggplant and save the rest to pour over the salad. Arrange the tomatoes, rocket, shallot, dressed eggplant and crisp flat bread on a large platter. Pour the reserved dressing over and scatter over the goat's cheese.

PREP AHEAD

The dressing, roasted eggplant and crisp bread can all be prepared on the morning of serving. Reheat the eggplant in a non-stick frying pan over gentle heat.

THE SKINNY

Roasting eggplant uses much less oil than pan-frying and you get a crisper result. Only a small amount of goat's cheese is used but you still get to enjoy the creamy taste.

Baby leaf salad with roasted beetroot, sugared almonds and crisp jamón

preparation time 20 minutes / cooking time 35 minutes / serves 4

It's the extra bits you add to a salad that make it special. Sugared almonds and crisp bits of jamón raise the bar for this roasted beetroot and leaf salad. If you have access to Marcona almonds from Spain, then use them. They're starting to appear in many delis and supermarkets and are considered the best almonds in the world.

4–5 baby beetroot (beets), scrubbed
   and trimmed
1 teaspoon extra virgin olive oil
2 slices jamón (serrano ham)
   or prosciutto (Parma ham)
4 handfuls mixed baby lettuce leaves
1 head red witlof (chicory/Belgian
   endive), leaves separated

Sugared almonds
3 tablespoons blanched almonds,
   roughly chopped
1 tablespoon honey
1 teaspoon extra virgin olive oil
1 tablespoon caster (superfine) sugar

Dressing
1 tablespoon sherry vinegar
2½ tablespoons extra virgin olive oil
1 teaspoon Dijon mustard

Preheat the oven to 180°C (350°F/Gas 4). Cut the beetroot into quarters and place on a baking tray. Drizzle over the olive oil and season with sea salt and freshly ground black pepper. Roast for 25 minutes or until tender and caramelised.

To make the sugared almonds, place the almonds on a baking tray lined with baking paper. Drizzle with the honey and olive oil, sprinkle over the sugar and season with salt. Stir to evenly coat, then bake for 10 minutes or until golden. Remove and allow to cool.

Heat a non-stick frying pan over medium–high heat and cook the jamón for 1 minute each side or until crisp. Cool and break into pieces.

To make the dressing, place all the ingredients in a small glass jar with a lid, season and shake well.

Place the leaves on plates or in a big bowl. Arrange the beetroot, crisp jamón and sugared almonds on top. Drizzle over the dressing and serve.

PREP AHEAD

The nuts, dressing and beetroot can all be made 1 day ahead and the salad assembled just before eating.

THE SKINNY

Nuts, ham, salami and cheese make salads infinitely more appealing but obviously they are higher on the fat scale. By using just a little, you still get the taste and texture but not so many calories.

Turkey and watercress salad with poppy seed vinaigrette

preparation time 10 minutes / serves 4

This has everything you want in a big salad: rainbow-coloured veggies, zingy dressing and some sustenance to keep you full. As an added bonus, it also contains more than three of your five a day. Use a julienne tool or hand-held mandolin to easily cut the carrots. Watercress is a little more peppery than spinach but you can use either.

150 g (5½ oz) picked watercress, roughly chopped
1 red capsicum (pepper), cut into matchsticks
2 large carrots, cut into matchsticks
2 tablespoons crumbled feta cheese
300 g (10½ oz) turkey meat, shredded or sliced

Poppy seed vinaigrette
2 small French shallots (eschalots), finely chopped
3 tablespoons honey
2 tablespoons apple cider vinegar
2 tablespoons vegetable oil
2 teaspoons Dijon mustard
2 teaspoons poppy seeds

To make the poppy seed vinaigrette, place all the ingredients in a blender except the poppy seeds. Blend well and add some sea salt and freshly ground black pepper. Transfer to a bowl and stir in the poppy seeds.

Layer the watercress, capsicum, carrot, feta, then the turkey in a large shallow bowl. Cover and refrigerate until using. Pour over enough dressing to coat the salad just before serving.

PREP AHEAD

The chopped ingredients will keep refrigerated for 2 days but dress just before serving.

THE SKINNY

This is another great 'packed lunch' salad that will keep for days. The dressing uses very little oil and the flavour comes from the honey, mustard and lemon juice.

Crab, spinach and avocado salad with Tabasco-lime dressing

preparation time 10 minutes / cooking time 5 minutes / serves 4

Who doesn't adore fresh crab? Briny white flakes that smell like the sea is my idea of nirvana. But, if it's not available or in season, tinned white crabmeat is better than you think. It's comparable to good tinned tuna and much easier on the budget. Although crab doesn't need much company to make it taste good, a Tabasco-spiked dressing and crisp breadcrumbs make this spinach salad a step up from the ordinary.

2 handfuls fresh chunky breadcrumbs
olive oil spray
150 g (5½ oz) baby spinach
1 ripe avocado, cut into chunks
200 g (7 oz) cherry tomatoes, halved
4 spring onions (scallions), thinly sliced
100 g (3½ oz) crabmeat

Tabasco-lime dressing
juice of 2 limes
3 tablespoons extra virgin olive oil
1 tablespoon red wine vinegar
1 teaspoon Tabasco or hot sauce
1 tablespoon honey

Preheat the oven to 200°C (400°F/Gas 6). Spread the breadcrumbs evenly on a baking tray. Spray with a little olive oil and season with sea salt and freshly ground black pepper. Bake for 5 minutes or until golden and crisp.

Arrange the spinach, avocado, tomato, spring onion and crabmeat on a platter.

To make the Tabasco-lime dressing, mix all the ingredients together in a small bowl and season. Pour over enough dressing to coat the salad and, when ready to eat, scatter with the crisp breadcrumbs.

PREP AHEAD

The crisp breadcrumbs and dressing can be made 1 day ahead and the salad can be made and refrigerated 4 hours ahead. Dress and scatter with the breadcrumbs just before serving.

THE SKINNY

Croûtons or crisp breadcrumbs won't be so caloric if you use an olive oil spray. The dressing relies more on lime juice than oil, keeping it skinny.

Beetroot, pea and feta salad with dill and honey-mustard vinaigrette

preparation time 10 minutes / cooking time 20 minutes / serves 4

This fetching green and purple vegetable salad is tossed with an apple cider vinegar based dressing and topped with a whisper of salty feta cheese. It's satisfying on its own, or great alongside grilled lamb or steak.

4 beetroot (beets), scrubbed
  and trimmed
200 g (7 oz) sugar snap peas, roughly
  chopped
100 g (3½ oz) fresh or frozen
  shelled peas
3 teaspoons chopped dill
25 g (1 oz) feta cheese, crumbled

Honey-mustard vinaigrette
2 tablespoons apple cider vinegar
2 tablespoons extra virgin olive oil
1 tablespoon wholegrain mustard
2 teaspoons honey

Place the beetroot in a large saucepan of lightly salted water and bring to the boil. Reduce the heat to medium and simmer for 20–25 minutes or until tender when pierced with the tip of a knife. Drain the beetroot and, when cool enough to handle, cut into 3 cm (1¼ inch) cubes and place in a bowl.

Meanwhile, make the honey-mustard vinaigrette. Place all the ingredients in a small glass jar with a lid, season with sea salt and freshly ground black pepper and shake well. Pour half over the warm beetroot and mix well.

Slice the sugar snaps in half lengthways. Blanch them along with the peas for 1 minute in lightly salted boiling water. Rinse in cold water, drain well and add to the beetroot along with the dill.

Pour the remaining dressing over and scatter with the feta. Don't stir too much because the beetroot tends to turn everything purple — just scoop up and serve.

PREP AHEAD

The vegetables and dressing can be prepared 1 day ahead and refrigerated separately. Mix together before serving.

THE SKINNY

The small amount of feta cheese injects a salty taste but not a huge amount of calories. If you want to make this more substantial, eat with smoked fish or grilled meat.

Vietnamese chicken salad

preparation time 10 minutes / cooking time 20 minutes / serves 4

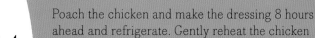

This is a very popular street-food dish in Vietnam. The Vietnamese boil an entire chicken, pick the bones clean, then toss the warm meat with a lime-chilli dressing and chopped peanuts. Poaching transforms the chicken into velvety shreds. When dressed warm with the sweet and sour lime dressing there is only one word to describe it: unbelievable. I've taken a short cut by using breast fillets, which are easier than using a whole bird. You could even use a warm barbecued chicken from the supermarket.

3 small chicken breast fillets, skin on
2 Lebanese (short) cucumbers
1 small red onion, halved
   and thinly sliced
1 large handful basil leaves
1 large handful mint leaves
1 large handful coriander (cilantro)
   leaves
1 thumb-sized red chilli, seeds removed
   and thinly sliced
2 tablespoons roasted peanuts, chopped

Lime dressing
juice of 3 limes
1 garlic clove, crushed
1 tablespoon fish sauce
1 tablespoon soft brown sugar

Bring a large saucepan of water to the boil. Add the chicken breasts, cover with a lid, turn off the heat and leave on the stove for 20 minutes. Remove the chicken, discard the skin and carefully shred the meat into a bowl.

Meanwhile, make the lime dressing. Mix all the ingredients together until the sugar has dissolved.

Use a vegetable peeler to peel the cucumber into ribbons. Add to the chicken. Add the onion, herbs, chilli and dressing and gently toss to combine. Serve scattered with the peanuts.

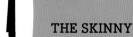

PREP AHEAD

Poach the chicken and make the dressing 8 hours ahead and refrigerate. Gently reheat the chicken to serve.

THE SKINNY

South-East Asian dressings are perfect because they don't involve a drop of oil. Poaching is brilliant because meat stays moist and, again, no oil is required.

Brown rice salad with poached chicken, broccoli and miso dressing

preparation time 15 minutes / cooking time 20 minutes / serves 4–6

Although this one-meal salad sounds too chaste to be good, it has remarkable taste and texture. The punchy miso-mirin dressing is a pure hit of Japanese taste, while the green vegetables add crunch and goodness. Brown basmati is a little chewier than white so use whichever you prefer. Sesame seeds or chilli powder are nice sprinkled over as well.

200 g (7 oz/1 cup) brown basmati rice

1 litre (35 fl oz/4 cups) chicken stock
   or water

3 small skinless chicken breast fillets

200 g (7 oz) broccoli, cut into small
   florets

100 g (3½ oz) shelled frozen edamame
   (soya beans)

2 celery stalks, from the heart,
   thinly sliced

6 spring onions (scallions), very thinly
   sliced on the diagonal

Miso dressing

2 tablespoons rice vinegar

2 tablespoons mirin

1 tablespoon red miso paste

2 teaspoons finely grated ginger

Place the rice in a small saucepan, add enough water to cover by 6 cm (2½ inches) and bring to the boil. Reduce the heat to medium–low and simmer for 15–20 minutes or until al dente. Drain and keep warm.

While the rice is cooking, place the stock or water in a saucepan and bring to the boil. Add the chicken breasts, cover with a lid, turn off the heat and leave to sit for 20 minutes. Remove the chicken and cut into slices.

Blanch the broccoli and edamame in salted boiling water, drain and rinse under cold water.

To make the miso dressing, mix all the ingredients together in a small bowl. Thin with a little water if it's too thick.

Spread the rice on a platter and top with the chicken and all the vegetables. Pour the dressing over and top with the spring onion.

PREP AHEAD

The entire salad can be prepared 1 day ahead and refrigerated but not assembled until serving.

THE SKINNY

Miso is a star dressing ingredient as it has so much flavour and no oil is needed; the vinegar and mirin thin and balance out its intense saltiness. Use red or yellow miso in this dish for the best results.

Latin palm heart salad with orange, prawns and avocado

preparation time 20 minutes / serves 4

Palm hearts glam up any leaves with their artichoke-like flavour. They're particularly good in Latin or Italian salads with a bit of avocado. Store a few tins in your cupboard for an instant starter or special side salad. Most supermarkets sell them in the tinned vegetable aisle.

2 large navel oranges
1 bunch watercress, leaves picked
1 x 400 g (14 oz) tin hearts of palm, drained and sliced
1 avocado, chopped into 3 cm (1¼ inch) pieces
16 cooked prawns (shrimp), peeled and deveined
4 spring onions (scallions), chopped

Dressing
2 tablespoons lime juice
2 tablespoons vegetable oil
2 tablespoons honey
1 tablespoon red wine vinegar
1 teaspoon finely chopped coriander (cilantro)

Use a sharp knife to cut the peel off the oranges, then cut each lengthways into 4 slices. Drain on paper towel. Place the watercress, palm hearts, avocado, prawns, spring onion and orange in a large bowl or on a platter.

To make the dressing, place all the ingredients in a small glass jar with a lid, season with sea salt and freshly ground black pepper and shake well. Pour over the salad just before serving.

PREP AHEAD

The dressing can be made in the morning and the salad can be chopped up a couple of hours in advance. If doing so, toss the avocado with a little lemon or lime juice to keep it from discolouring.

THE SKINNY

Peeled cooked prawns are low in calories and full of protein, making them ideal to beef up a salad. Keep a bag on hand in your freezer to use as a quick addition to salads.

Puy lentil salad with walnuts, apple and blue cheese vinaigrette

preparation time 30 minutes / cooking time 25 minutes / serves 4

Walnuts, blue cheese and apple go together, no doubt about it. Whether on their own, or mixed with lentils or chicory, it's a winning salty, nutty and tart trio. Only a small amount of the cheese is mixed into the vinaigrette, giving you all the taste but not huge amounts of fat.

250 g (9 oz) Puy (tiny blue-green) lentils
1 litre (35 fl oz/4 cups) chicken stock
   or water
1 celery heart, finely chopped
1 granny smith apple, peeled, cored
   and roughly chopped
2 French shallots (eschalots), finely diced
4 tablespoons walnuts, toasted
   and chopped
2 tablespoons finely chopped flat-leaf
   (Italian) parsley

Blue cheese vinaigrette
2 tablespoons extra virgin olive oil
   or walnut oil
2 tablespoons red wine vinegar
1 tablespoon crumbled strong blue
   cheese, such as Roquefort
1 teaspoon Dijon mustard
1 garlic clove

Place the lentils and stock or water in a large saucepan and bring to the boil. Reduce the heat to low and simmer for 20–25 minutes or until al dente. Drain and pour into a bowl. Add the celery, apple, shallot, walnuts and parsley.

To make the blue cheese vinaigrette, place all the ingredients in a small glass jar with a lid, season with sea salt and freshly ground black pepper and shake well. Remove the garlic clove just before serving. Pour the dressing over the salad and toss well.

PREP AHEAD

This can be made in full and kept covered and refrigerated for 2–3 days, but hold back the parsley until serving.

THE SKINNY

Blue cheese is strong in taste, so only a little is needed to make the dressing come to life.

Baby greens with goat's cheese, dried cherries and sugared hazelnuts

preparation time 15 minutes / cooking time 5 minutes / serves 4

Walnut oil and fruit vinegar make dreamy dressings for baby salad leaves. Slender green beans, sugared nuts and goat's cheese get tossed along with it for a special side salad or starter. Always remember to keep hazelnut or walnut oils in the refrigerator because they go off very quickly if not kept chilled.

100 g (3½ oz) thin green beans trimmed
  (if big, halve lengthways)
150 g (5¼ oz) mixed baby salad leaves
  (mesclun)
2 tablespoons dried cherries,
  roughly chopped
5 spring onions (scallions), sliced
50 g (1¾ oz) hard goat's cheese,
  crumbled

Raspberry and nut-oil dressing

1 tablespoon raspberry
  or balsamic vinegar
3 tablespoons hazelnut or walnut oil
1 teaspoon Dijon mustard
1 garlic clove, bruised

Sugared hazelnuts

3 tablespoons hazelnuts, halved
  or roughly chopped
1 heaped tablespoon icing
  (confectioners') sugar

To make the sugared hazelnuts, preheat the oven to 180°C (350°F/Gas 4). Rinse the hazelnuts in water and toss with the icing sugar and a little sea salt. Spread over an oiled baking tray and bake for 5 minutes or until crisp. Scrape off the tray and set aside to cool.

Meanwhile, blanch the green beans for 1 minute in salted boiling water, drain, rinse in cold water and dry. Place in a large bowl and add the leaves, cherries, spring onion and sugared hazelnuts.

To make the raspberry nut-oil dressing, place all the ingredients in a small glass jar with a lid, season with sea salt and freshly ground black pepper and shake well.

Pour over enough dressing to coat the salad and scatter over the goat's cheese.

PREP AHEAD

The nuts, blanched beans and dressing can be made 1 day ahead and refrigerated separately.

THE SKINNY

The tiny quantity of nuts keeps the calories down but makes the salad a bit more special. You could also add grilled (broiled) sliced lean steak or grill the goat's cheese on a slice of toasted baguette to make it more substantial.

Potato and smoked trout salad with capers and wholegrain mustard

preparation time 20 minutes / cooking time 10 minutes / serves 4

Here is an inspired way to get your omega-3 and -6 vitamins. Smoked fish such as trout and mackerel are 'super' or 'power' foods because they are high in these vital oils

800 g (1 lb 12 oz) red-skinned potatoes
1 tablespoon red wine vinegar
2 teaspoons finely chopped dill
1 tablespoon baby capers in brine,
    drained and rinsed
1 small red onion, thinly sliced
    into half moons
4 handfuls picked watercress
150 g (5½ oz) smoked trout or mackerel
    fillets, skin and bones removed,
    flesh broken into chunks

Dressing
2 tablespoons wholegrain mustard
2 tablespoons red wine vinegar
2 tablespoons extra virgin olive oil
1 teaspoon caster (superfine) sugar

Place the potatoes in a saucepan of lightly salted water and bring to the boil. Simmer for 10 minutes or until tender when pierced with the tip of a knife, then drain. When cool enough to handle, peel and cut into thick slices. Place in a bowl and toss with the vinegar and some sea salt and freshly ground black pepper.

To make the dressing, mix all the ingredients together in a small bowl. Pour over the potato and add the dill, capers and onion. Arrange the salad on plates with a handful of the watercress, then top with the smoked trout.

PREP AHEAD

This can be made 1 day ahead; add the toppings just before serving.

THE SKINNY

Smoked fish such as trout and mackerel are powerhouses for health and are a great protein to add to salads. Dress the potato salad while warm to let the flavours soak in.

Chopped tarragon, bacon and chicken salad

preparation time 15 minutes / cooking time 5 minutes / serves 4

If you have leftover chicken, this salad tossed in a French vinaigrette is a clever solution. Alternatively, you can buy a barbecued chicken and shred the meat. It's a bit like a cobb salad but all mixed together.

3 lean bacon slices
1 large avocado, cut into small chunks
300 g (3½ oz) shredded barbecued or poached chicken
150 g (5½ oz) cherry tomatoes, halved
1 celery heart, thinly sliced
2 teaspoons chopped tarragon
5 spring onions (scallions), thinly sliced
100 g (3½ oz) fresh or frozen shelled peas, blanched

Dressing
3 tablespoons extra virgin olive oil
2 tablespoons white balsamic or wine vinegar
1 tablespoon Dijon mustard
pinch of white sugar

Heat a non-stick frying pan over medium–high heat until very hot. Add the bacon and cook until golden and crisp. Remove and drain on paper towel. It should be crisp enough to crumble easily.

To make the dressing, mix all the ingredients with a pinch of sea salt in a small bowl.

Place the avocado, chicken, tomato, celery, tarragon, spring onion, peas and bacon in a large bowl. Pour over the dressing and toss gently to combine.

PREP AHEAD

The salad can be made 4 hours ahead, dressed and refrigerated.

THE SKINNY

Bacon is high on the fat scale so the idea is to just have a little taste of it. Chicken keeps you full, making this a healthy one-dish meal that won't leave you hankering for a snack a few hours later.

Sushi salad with seared tuna, avocado and rice wine dressing

preparation time 20 minutes / cooking time 15 minutes / serves 4

If you love sushi but can't be bothered rolling it, this is the ticket. Just pay close attention when cooking the rice; besides that, it's an assembly job. This past year
I finally relented to buying a rice cooker and it's one appliance that never gathers dust. The rice always comes out perfect and you don't need to babysit it while cooking.

300 g (10½ oz) sushi rice, rinsed
   3 times until the water runs clear
330 ml (11¼ fl oz/1⅓ cups) water
75 ml (2⅜ fl oz) rice vinegar
2 tablespoons caster (superfine) sugar
500 g (1 lb 2 oz) piece of tuna fillet
   or 2 thick tuna steaks
cooking oil spray
1 sheet nori (seaweed), shredded
1 avocado, sliced
1 small red onion, thinly sliced
   into half moons
1 tablespoon black or white sesame
   seeds, toasted

Place the rice and water in a saucepan, cover and bring to the boil. Reduce the heat to low and simmer for 12 minutes or until the water is absorbed. Remove from the heat and leave covered for 10 minutes.

Place the vinegar, sugar and a pinch of salt in a small saucepan over medium heat, stirring to dissolve the sugar. Remove from the heat.

Season the tuna liberally with freshly ground black pepper, spray with a little oil and sear in a non-stick frying pan over very high heat for 1 minute each side. Remove and allow to cool.

Spread the hot rice in a large glass baking dish or plastic tray. Drizzle two-thirds of the rice vinegar dressing over and gently mix using a spatula. Add the shredded nori and mix again. Spoon the rice onto plates.

Slice the tuna and place over each serving. Add the avocado and onion and sprinkle with the sesame seeds. Serve with a bowl of the remaining rice vinegar dressing to pass around.

PREP AHEAD

Sushi rice doesn't taste good refrigerated so it's better to cool it quickly and leave it covered at room temperature. Make it 2 hours ahead. The fish can be seared and sliced about 8 hours ahead and refrigerated.

THE SKINNY

Seared fish and rice is the perfect one-dish meal and with all of the extra toppings you won't feel deprived. With the exception of the oil to coat the fish, there is no other fat.

Tuna pasta salad with peppadews, basil and balsamic dressing

preparation time 20 minutes / cooking time 10 minutes / serves 4

There isn't a drop of mayonnaise in sight here. Frankly, it's just not needed with all the flavour components such as pickled peppers, capers and sweet balsamic dressing. Orecchiette is great in pasta salads because of its thickness. They won't go soggy and their little pockets tuck in all the tasty bits. Peppadews are little red cherry peppers that are pickled. They are similar to Italian pepperoncini but less spicy. Sold all over the world in supermarkets, they perk up salads and burgers and they're delicious as part of an antipasti platter.

350 g (12 oz) orecchiette (little ears) pasta
2 x 185 g (6½ oz) tins tuna in brine, drained and flaked
1 tablespoon baby capers
1 celery heart, chopped
1 small red onion, finely diced
2 tablespoons finely chopped basil
15 pickled red cherry peppers (peppadews), chopped
rocket (arugula) leaves and halved cherry tomatoes, to serve (optional)

Balsamic dressing
3 tablespoons balsamic vinegar
3 tablespoons extra virgin olive oil
1 teaspoon caster (superfine) sugar

Cook the pasta in salted boiling water for 10 minutes or until al dente. Drain, rinse in cold water and drain again. Pour into a large bowl and add the tuna, capers, celery, onion, basil and peppadews.

To make the balsamic dressing, place all the ingredients in a small glass jar with a lid, season with sea salt and freshly ground black pepper and shake well.

Pour over the pasta and mix well. Add the rocket and cherry tomatoes to up the vegetable factor if you like.

PREP AHEAD

This salad will keep for 3 days, covered in the refrigerator. You may want to add the rocket and tomatoes a bit later to keep them fresher.

THE SKINNY

With the exception of the celery and basil, nearly all the ingredients here are cupboard staples. It's wise to have a well-stocked pantry so you can make skinny salads on the fly. The balsamic dressing pumps up the taste without mayonnaise or excess oil.

Rice noodle salad with turkey, carrot and lime-chilli dressing

preparation time 20 minutes / cooking time 10 minutes / serves 4

This makes a great cold packed lunch for work, as the ingredients stand up well to the dressing for a long time. Chicken breast can be used in place of the turkey, just pulse it in the food processor until minced.

100 g (3¼ oz) dried thin rice noodles
1 thumb-sized red chilli, seeds removed
    and cut into thin slices
2 carrots, shredded
1 small red onion, thinly sliced
    into half moons
1 handful coriander (cilantro) leaves,
    roughly chopped
1 handful mint leaves, roughly chopped
cooking oil spray
500 g (1 lb 2 oz) minced (ground)
    turkey

Lime-chilli dressing
2 tablespoons fish sauce
2 tablespoons soft brown sugar
juice of 4 small limes
1 garlic clove, crushed

Pour boiling water over the noodles and allow to sit for 5 minutes. Drain, rinse under cold water and place in a large bowl, along with the chilli, carrot, onion and herbs.

To make the lime-chilli dressing, mix all the ingredients together.

Heat a non-stick frying pan or wok over high heat until extremely hot. Lightly coat with oil and cook the minced turkey until it is nicely browned, then break into chunks. Add to the noodle mixture, pour over the dressing and mix well.

PREP AHEAD

The entire salad can be prepared 1 day ahead, covered and refrigerated.

THE SKINNY

Minced turkey is much lower in fat than pork, which is normally used in a salad such as this. With virtuous meat and a tasty oil-free dressing, this makes a spectacular lean lunch.

Beef, radicchio and mushroom salad with lemon-parmesan dressing

preparation time 20 minutes / cooking time 10 minutes / resting time 10 minutes / serves 4

Bitter radicchio and crisp celery join forces with velvety beef and mushrooms, and it all gets tossed in a sharp lemon-parmesan dressing.

150 g (5½ oz) chestnut or button
   mushrooms, very thinly sliced
1 celery heart, very thinly sliced
2 large handfuls radicchio
   or 1 small head red witlof
   (chicory/Belgian endive), sliced
100 g (3½ oz) cherry tomatoes, halved
200 g (7 oz) beef fillet or rump steak,
   trimmed of all fat
1 teaspoon extra virgin olive oil

Lemon-parmesan dressing
3 tablespoons extra virgin olive oil
2 tablespoons finely grated parmesan
2 teaspoons caster (superfine) sugar
finely grated zest and juice of 2 lemons
1 garlic clove, bruised

Place the mushrooms, celery, radicchio and tomato in a bowl. Rub the beef with the olive oil and season with sea salt and freshly ground black pepper.

Heat a non-stick frying pan over very high heat until very hot and sear the beef for about 2 minutes each side. Remove and let sit for 10 minutes, then thinly slice. Add to the bowl of salad.

To make the dressing, place all the ingredients in a small glass jar with a lid, season with sea salt and freshly ground black pepper and shake well. Keep the garlic back when pouring the dressing over the salad. Toss gently and serve.

PREP AHEAD

Grill and slice the steak, and make the dressing 1 day ahead, but chop the other ingredients a couple of hours in advance and mix just before serving.

THE SKINNY

Beef satiates you like no other protein. It doesn't have to be caloric if you buy a lean cut such as rump or fillet. Trim any excess fat before slicing. Only a small amount of parmesan is used but the nutty taste still comes through the dressing.

Iceberg wedges with Japanese ginger-onion dressing

preparation time 15 minutes / serves 4

Whenever I eat at a Japanese restaurant I always order this type of salad. For years I have been messing about trying to recreate the ginger dressing. After many revisions I think this is pretty close. It looks like a long list of ingredients but it all goes in the blender and gets puréed. Make as a starter or side or transform it into a one-dish meal with some grilled steak or tuna.

1 head iceberg lettuce or 4 baby gem
  lettuces, halved
2 beefsteak (oxheart) tomatoes,
  cut into wedges
2 carrots, shredded
1 small cucumber, thinly sliced

Japanese ginger-onion dressing
2 tablespoons rice wine vinegar
2 tablespoons soy sauce
2 tablespoons white sugar
1 tablespoon tomato paste
  (concentrated purée)
1 tablespoon vegetable oil
1 tablespoon water
2 teaspoons chopped fresh ginger
1 tablespoon finely chopped
  white onion
½ celery stalk, chopped

To make the Japanese ginger-onion dressing, place all the ingredients in a blender or food processor and process until smooth, then pour into a small jug.

Cut the lettuce into 4 wedges and remove any soft outer leaves. Place a wedge on each plate. Arrange the tomato, carrot and cucumber alongside. Just before serving, pour over enough dressing to coat the salad.

PREP AHEAD

The dressing can be made 1 day ahead but keep it in a glass jar with a lid so you can shake it again before pouring.

THE SKINNY

This ginger and rice wine vinegar dressing has so much punch but only 1 tablespoon of oil. You certainly won't feel like you're missing out.

Soups for
Dinner or To Start

Shabu shabu beef and vegetable soup

preparation time 10 minutes / freezing time 15 minutes / cooking time 10 minutes / serves 4

Traditionally this soup is served in a hotpot and the various vegetables, meat and noodles are dipped into the hot stock, then eaten with soy or sesame sauces. I have taken great liberties in combining the beef and vegetables into the soup base. You can add cooked udon noodles to the finished soup, but the soup is already quite satisfying for such a simple combination.

160 g (5⅝ oz) beef fillet or rump steak, trimmed of all fat
1 litre (35 fl oz/4 cups) beef, chicken or vegetable stock
3 tablespoons ponzu sauce
3 tablespoons mirin
1 large onion, halved and thinly sliced
2 small carrots, peeled and cut into 1.5 cm (⅝ inch) pieces
2 baby leeks, white part only, thinly sliced
75 g (2⅝ oz) savoy cabbage, finely shredded
2 spring onions (scallions), thinly sliced
1 tablespoon sesame seeds, toasted

Place the beef in the freezer for 15 minutes or longer if you can. You just want it firm but not frozen. When firm, use your sharpest knife to cut it into very thin slices and set aside. You can also ask a butcher to do this for you, or Japanese supermarkets sell beef already sliced.

Bring the stock to the simmer in a saucepan and pour in the ponzu and mirin. Add the onion, carrot, leek and cabbage and simmer for 7–8 minutes or until tender but still firm. Divide the beef among serving bowls, pour in the soup and serve immediately, sprinkled with spring onion and sesame seeds.

PREP AHEAD

This soup is best made just before serving so the vegetables remain fresh and al dente.

THE SKINNY

Poaching all the ingredients requires no oil at all and the ponzu and mirin add immense flavour to the stock.

Quick prawn noodle soup with fresh herbs

preparation time 15 minutes / cooking time 10 minutes / serves 4

Pho is the heart-and-soul noodle soup of Vietnam. You'll find a street vendor practically on every corner selling it with people hunched over, slurping up noodles. Here it's made with prawns, but you can use chopped beef, pork or chicken. Just add your favourite meat to the stock base, aromatic with hints of ginger, star anise and cinnamon. The fresh herbs and chilli sauce make it an eating experience and no other dishes are needed. Fresh bean sprouts are also a nice addition and give it a little crunch.

200 g (7 oz) dried thick rice noodles
1 litre (35 fl oz/4 cups) chicken
   or vegetable stock
1 tablespoon fish sauce
juice of 2 limes
5 cm (2 inch) piece of ginger,
   cut into slices
1 cinnamon stick
2 star anise
pinch of white sugar
16 raw small prawns (shrimp), peeled
   and deveined with tails left on
6 spring onions (scallions), thinly sliced
2 handfuls basil leaves
2 handfuls mint leaves
2 handfuls coriander (cilantro) leaves
Vietnamese or Chinese chilli sauce,
   to serve

Cook the noodles in a saucepan of boiling water for 3–5 minutes or until al dente and drain. Divide among bowls.

Meanwhile, heat the stock in a saucepan and add the fish sauce, lime juice, ginger, cinnamon, star anise and sugar. Bring to the boil, then add the prawns and simmer gently for 2 minutes.

Divide the prawns among the bowls and pour the soup over the top. Top with the spring onion and herbs. Serve with the chilli sauce on the side for stirring through.

PREP AHEAD

The base for this soup can be made 1 week ahead, then strained and refrigerated or frozen. Don't add the noodles, prawns and fresh herbs until just before serving.

THE SKINNY

No oil here, and the lime, ginger and spice–infused broth is a mouth-watering base for the noodles and prawns.

Celeriac and roasted garlic soup with chives

preparation time 15 minutes / cooking time 50 minutes / serves 4

Celeriac or celery root as it's sometimes called, is one of my favourite winter root vegetables. Its starchy nature makes it an ideal ingredient for soup or mash. Roasted garlic and celery salt inject a little more pizzazz for a very comforting thick soup.

1 bulb garlic
1½ tablespoons olive oil
1 large onion, chopped
2 celery stalks, finely diced
½ teaspoon celery salt
½ large celeriac, peeled and chopped
   (about 250 g/9 oz peeled)
1 litre (35 fl oz/4 cups) vegetable stock
½ bunch chives, finely chopped

Preheat the oven to 190°C (375°F/Gas 5). Cut the top third off the bulb of garlic and discard. Drizzle the remaining garlic with ½ tablespoon of the olive oil. Season with sea salt and freshly ground black pepper, wrap in foil and roast for 40 minutes or until tender.

Meanwhile, heat the remaining olive oil in a large saucepan over medium–high heat. Add the onion, celery and celery salt, season with pepper and cook for 8 minutes or until the onion is translucent. Add the celeriac and stock, partially cover, reduce the heat to low and simmer for 40 minutes or until the celeriac is tender.

When the garlic is ready, squeeze the cloves into the soup. Purée everything in a food processor or blender until smooth. Season to taste, then pour into large bowls and scatter over the chives.

PREP AHEAD

The soup can be made up to 2 days ahead and refrigerated or frozen.

THE SKINNY

You won't need as much oil to cook the onions and vegetables if you turn down the heat a bit lower; they will sweat slowly but you get the same result. All the ingredients here are pure goodness with hardly any fat.

Chicken, rice and chunky vegetable soup with mini parmesan croûtons

preparation time 15 minutes / cooking time 30 minutes / serves 4

My mother Louise made a legendary chicken soup that my sisters and I have always struggled to replicate. She would slowly poach a whole bird, and when it was finished, shower it with decadent fried croûtons rolled in parmesan. I started this recipe with her masterpiece in mind but have changed things a bit. This lightning-quick method uses chicken breast and vegetables poached in a hot stock, which keeps everything juicy, and I've given the croûtons a skinny makeover — they're baked in olive oil and parmesan.

1 litre (35 fl oz/4 cups) good-quality chicken or vegetable stock
2 skinless chicken breast fillets
4 carrots, cut into 2 cm (¾ inch) chunks
1 small celery heart with leaves, sliced into 2 cm (¾ inch) pieces
1 brown onion, cut into large dice
60 g (2¼ oz/⅓ cup) basmati rice
100 g (3½ oz/1¼ cup) frozen or fresh shelled peas
2 tablespoons flat-leaf (Italian) parsley, finely chopped

Croûtons
2 slices sourdough bread, cut into 1 cm (½ inch) cubes
1 teaspoon olive oil
1 tablespoon grated parmesan

Preheat the oven to 200°C (400°F/Gas 6).

Bring the stock to the boil in a saucepan, then add the chicken. Add the chicken and simmer gently for 4 minutes. Add the carrot, celery and onion, turn off the heat but leave the pan on the stove and cover with a lid. Leave to sit for 25 minutes.

Meanwhile, boil the rice in plenty of water until al dente. Drain and set aside.

To make the croûtons, place the bread on a baking tray, toss in the oil, parmesan and some sea salt and freshly ground black pepper. Bake for 6 minutes or until golden and crisp. Remove and allow to cool.

Remove the chicken from the stock and shred with two forks. Add the meat back to the stock, along with the peas, rice and parsley. Turn the heat back on to high and heat for a few minutes to warm the peas through. Serve in bowls with the croûtons scattered over.

PREP AHEAD

The soup can be made up to 3 days ahead and stored in the fridge. Store the croûtons separately.

THE SKINNY

Since everything is freshly poached in the soup, no oil is needed. The croûtons only have a tiny bit of cheese and oil and lend the soup a salty, nutty kick.

Chipotle black bean soup with lime-pickled onion

preparation time 10 minutes / cooking time 25 minutes / serves 4

It's good to be able to reach into your cupboard and pull out enough ingredients to make soup and this is one of those types of soups. Although in a perfect world I'd like to soak my own beans, I never have the time. Tinned beans work just as well and soak up all the aromatic spices. Tart lime-marinated onions top off the soup for a great combination. If you own a mandolin, use it to slice the onions paper thin.

1 tablespoon olive oil
4 garlic cloves, finely chopped
2 red onions, thinly sliced
1 tablespoon ground cumin
1 tablespoon smoked paprika
1 tablespoon chipotle purée
    or Tabasco sauce
2 x 400 g (14 oz) tins black beans,
    drained and rinsed
800 ml (28 fl oz) vegetable stock
juice of 2 limes
light sour cream, coriander (cilantro)
    leaves and crisp tortillas, to serve

Lime-pickled onion
juice of 2 limes
1 small red onion, thinly sliced

To make the lime-pickled onion, combine the lime juice and onion in a small non-reactive bowl and season with sea salt and freshly ground black pepper. Leave to pickle for 30 minutes.

Meanwhile, heat the olive oil in a saucepan over medium–high heat. Add the garlic and onion and season. Sauté for 8 minutes or until translucent. Add the spices and chipotle purée, cook for 1 minute, then add the beans, stock and lime juice. Simmer for 15 minutes, then purée. Pour everything back into a clean pan to reheat. Serve with a little of the drained pickled onion. Top with a small spoonful of sour cream and some coriander and the tortillas on the side.

PREP AHEAD

This can be made 2 days ahead but don't make the onions until the day of serving. This soup freezes well.

THE SKINNY

Beans are immensely healthy and 'stick to your ribs', keeping hunger pangs at bay. When paired with smoky chillies and lime, they transform into gorgeous soups and stews.

Vietnamese prawn, rice, tomato and dill soup

preparation time 10 minutes / cooking time 15 minutes / serves 4

Some Vietnamese dishes are so simple it doesn't seem possible. Because of their purity, they don't require many ingredients or complicated cooking. This was one of my favourite soups I experienced while there. Dill seems like a strange herb to use in Asia but because of the French occupation, copious amounts are used. This might sound like a lot of dill but it really works.

270 g (9½ oz/1⅛ cups) basmati rice, not rinsed
1.2 litres (44 fl oz) chicken stock
2 tablespoons fish sauce
6 cm (2½ inch) piece of ginger, peeled and shredded
juice of 2 limes
6 large roma (plum) tomatoes, seeds removed and diced
300 g (10½ oz) raw prawns (shrimp), peeled and deveined with tails left on
3 tablespoons chopped dill
1 small handful coriander (cilantro) leaves, roughly chopped

Place the rice in a small saucepan, add enough water to cover by 6 cm (2½ inches), cover with a lid and bring to the boil. Reduce the heat to medium–low and simmer for 8 minutes or until al dente. Drain and set aside.

Bring the stock to the boil in a large saucepan and add the cooked rice, fish sauce, ginger, lime juice, tomato, prawns and dill. Simmer for a few minutes until the prawns are cooked. Serve in bowls with the coriander scattered over.

PREP AHEAD

This is best prepared just before serving.

THE SKINNY

The rice and prawns keep this light soup filling and there isn't a drop of oil in sight.

Gazpacho with apple salsa

preparation time 10 minutes / chilling time 3 hours / serves 6

When the weather is steamy hot there is no other food that refreshes you like gazpacho, and with the addition of crisp sour granny smith apple, even more so. I never tire of it and there are endless ways to play around with this soup, whether it's adding chilli or using different coloured tomatoes. Ripe and tasty vegetables are a must for this, so summer is the best time to make it.

500 g (1 lb 2 oz) ripe juicy tomatoes
½ telegraph (long) or 2 Lebanese (short) cucumbers, peeled
1 white or red onion
1 yellow or red capsicum (pepper), seeds removed
2 tablespoons extra virgin olive oil, plus extra for drizzling
1 tablespoon sherry vinegar
1 teaspoon smoked Spanish paprika (pimentón)
2 thick slices white crusty bread, roughly torn
400 ml (14 fl oz) vegetable or chicken stock, chilled
1 granny smith apple

Roughly chop all the vegetables, reserving a small amount of each before chopping. Place the chopped vegetables, olive oil, vinegar, paprika, bread and stock in a food processor and season with sea salt. Purée until very smooth.

Finely dice the reserved vegetables to make about 1 cup of salsa. Core and finely dice the apple. Mix with the salsa and set aside. At this point you can chill the soup for 3 hours or pour immediately over cups of ice to serve. Scatter over the salsa mixture and drizzle with a bit of olive oil to serve.

PREP AHEAD

This can be made 1 day ahead and refrigerated.

THE SKINNY

Food doesn't get more healthy than this with blitzed raw veggies and stock. A little oil is used but it's quite minimal. Get your five-a-day with this icy treat.

Chilled crab, cucumber and yoghurt soup

preparation time 10 minutes / chilling time 2 hours / serves 4

There is not a truer saying than 'cool as a cucumber'. Their watery nature is pure refreshment when the weather's hot. Combined with yoghurt, Tabasco and spring onion, it makes a relishing chilly soup. Be sure to use cold stock because it can go sludgy if puréed with hot liquid. Make your stock and add some ice cubes to cool it quickly.

1 telegraph (long) or 2 Lebanese (short) cucumbers, peeled

1 small ripe avocado, cut into chunks

2 teaspoons Tabasco sauce

6 spring onions (scallions), thinly sliced

2 tablespoons chopped coriander (cilantro)

300 ml (10½ fl oz) vegetable stock, chilled

juice of 2 limes

100 g (3½ oz) low-fat plain yoghurt

100 g (3½ oz) crabmeat

Chop all but one-quarter of the cucumber into chunks. Place in a blender and add the avocado, 1½ teaspoons of the Tabasco sauce, half the spring onion and coriander, the stock, lime juice and yoghurt and season with sea salt and freshly ground black pepper. Blend until very smooth. Pour into a container and refrigerate for 2 hours or until chilled.

Remove the seeds from the remaining cucumber and finely dice the flesh. Place in a small bowl, add the crabmeat and the remaining Tabasco sauce, spring onion and coriander and combine. Set aside.

Pour the soup into bowls and top with a dollop of crab mixture before serving. Crack plenty of black pepper over.

PREP AHEAD

The soup is best made on the day otherwise the avocado will turn a greyish colour.

THE SKINNY

No oil is required to make this cold spicy soup any better.

Caramelised onion and fennel soup with cavolo nero and barley

preparation time 10 minutes / cooking time 30 minutes / serves 4

Caramelised onion soup is a winter treat. Here the traditional cheesy croûton has been replaced with greens and chewy barley to keep it full of goodness and flavour.

1 tablespoon olive oil
4 brown onions, thinly sliced
3 fennel bulbs, cores removed
   and thinly sliced
3 garlic cloves, chopped
1 teaspoon finely chopped rosemary
   or thyme
1 large pinch of caster (superfine) sugar
50 g (1¾ oz) farro or pearled barley
1 litre (35 fl oz/4 cups) vegetable stock
1 tablespoon brandy
100 g (3½ oz) cavolo nero (Tuscan
   black kale), stalks discarded and
   leaves thinly sliced
crusty bread, to serve

Heat the olive oil in a large saucepan over medium heat. Add the onion, fennel, garlic and rosemary and season well with sea salt, freshly ground black pepper and the sugar. Reduce the heat to low and cook for 20 minutes or until golden.

While the vegetables are cooking, bring a saucepan of salted water to the boil. Add the farro and cook for 10 minutes or until al dente, then drain.

When the vegetables are done, pour in the stock and brandy and bring to the boil. Add the cavolo nero and cook for 5 minutes, then add the farro. Taste for seasoning and serve in large bowls with some bread.

PREP AHEAD

The soup can be made 2 days ahead. It can be frozen but may need a little extra stock to thin it out on reheating because the farro absorbs some of it.

THE SKINNY

If you slowly sauté onions over low heat, very little oil is needed. Farro and barley are extremely good sources of fibre and they keep you full.

Chinese hot and sour mushroom soup

preparation time 15 minutes / soaking time 15 minutes / cooking time 10 minutes / serves 4

The Chinese consider hot foods, such as this, 'yang', and cold foods 'yin'. The yang is reputed to increase your energy, so if you feel tired, have a comforting bowl of this to get your system moving and your yin/yang balance back on track. It's important to use white pepper because it provides the 'hot' while the black vinegar delivers the signature sour taste.

8 dried shiitake mushrooms
1 tablespoon sesame oil
3 cm (1¼ inch) piece of ginger, cut into 6 slices
100 g (3½ oz) small chestnut or other mushrooms, sliced
1 litre (35 fl oz/4 cups) chicken or beef stock
50 g (1¾ oz) tinned bamboo shoots, drained, rinsed and cut into julienne
2 tablespoons light soy sauce
3 tablespoons Chinese black vinegar
½ teaspoon freshly ground white pepper
120 g (4¼ oz) firm tofu, drained and cut into 1 cm (½ inch) pieces
1 egg, lightly beaten
1 tablespoon water
1 tablespoon cornflour (cornstarch)
sliced spring onion (scallion), to serve

Soak the dried mushrooms in boiling water for 15 minutes, then drain and squeeze out the excess water. Remove the stems and finely chop the caps.

Heat the sesame oil in a large saucepan over medium–high heat. Add the ginger, all the mushrooms and sauté for 3 minutes or until browned at the edges. Add the stock and bring to the boil. Add the bamboo shoots, soy, vinegar, pepper and tofu.

Slowly pour the beaten egg into the soup while stirring.

Mix the water with the cornflour to make a paste. Pour into the soup and stir until it thickens. Serve in bowls with some spring onion scattered over.

PREP AHEAD

This can be made 1 day ahead and refrigerated.

THE SKINNY

With the exception of the egg and sesame oil, this is ideal skinny food. With the tofu as protein, it's a very satisfying meal.

Pea and watercress soup

preparation time 15 minutes / cooking time 15 minutes / serves 4

Whiz up this neon green soup in any season and serve warm or chilled. When fresh peas aren't in season, frozen peas are a versatile stand-in for soups, salads or stews. Their quality is remarkable and they remain a much brighter green than fresh ones. Watercress lends a peppery kick.

1 teaspoon olive oil
1 brown onion, chopped
1 small red-skinned potato,
    peeled and diced
700 g (1 lb 9 oz) frozen or fresh
    shelled peas
800 ml (28 fl oz) vegetable or
    chicken stock
200 g (7 oz) picked watercress,
    roughly chopped
2 tablespoons chopped mint
soft bread, to serve

Heat the olive oil in a saucepan over medium–high heat. Add the onion and potato, season with sea salt and freshly ground black pepper and sauté for 5 minutes or until softened. Add the peas and stock and bring to a simmer. Add the watercress and three-quarters of the mint and cook for another 10 minutes. Purée the mixture, in batches, in a food processor or blender. Pour back into the pan to reheat, or cover and refrigerate if serving chilled. Serve in big bowls with the remaining mint scattered over. Eat with a thick slice of soft bread to keep it substantial.

PREP AHEAD

The soup can be made 1 day ahead and refrigerated, and it freezes well too.

THE SKINNY

Peas are quite filling and a great freezer staple to make quick soups or purées.

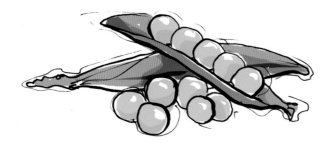

Tomato, chickpea and cumin soup

preparation time 10 minutes / cooking time 30 minutes / serves 4

This is another easy soup to pull together from your pantry. Cumin when left whole has a more pronounced flavour than ground and, along with the sweet cinnamon, makes this peasant-like soup subtle and aromatic.

2 tablespoons olive oil
1 large brown onion, chopped
1 large carrot, diced
2 garlic cloves, chopped
4 cm (1½ inch) piece of ginger, finely chopped
1 teaspoon cumin seeds
1 teaspoon smoked hot paprika
2 cinnamon sticks
500 ml (17 fl oz/2 cups) vegetable or chicken stock
1 x 400 g (14 oz) tin whole roma (plum) tomatoes
1 x 400 g (14 oz) tin chickpeas, drained and rinsed
finely grated zest and juice of 1 lemon

Heat the olive oil in a large saucepan over medium–high heat. Add the onion, carrot, garlic and ginger, season with sea salt and freshly ground black pepper and sauté for 8 minutes or until the vegetables have softened and are golden. Add the spices and cook for another minute. Pour in the stock, tomatoes and add a little more salt. Break up the tomatoes with a flat spoon. Cook for 15 minutes or until all the flavours come together. Add the chickpeas and lemon zest and juice and cook for another 5 minutes to warm through.

PREP AHEAD

The entire soup can be made 2 days ahead and refrigerated. It also freezes successfully.

THE SKINNY

Chickpeas are high in fibre, which, in addition to the ginger, onion and garlic, is supposed to keep your digestive system clean and healthy.

Weekday Dinners In Under One Hour

Spicy lamb kebabs with pomegranate seeds, herb salad and chilli sauce

preparation time 10 minutes / **cooking time** 5 minutes / **serves** 4

The sauce here sounds odd but, trust me, it really works. When dried red chilli or harissa is mixed with vinegar, it creates a wondrous sauce that isn't too spicy. The vinegar cuts the heat and balances out the flavours. The lamb skewers are marinated with it, then grilled and wrapped up with ruby pomegranate seeds, fresh herbs and Greek yoghurt for a mouth-watering kebab.

500 g (1 lb 2 oz) piece of bonelss
    lamb leg, trimmed of all fat
3 tablespoons harissa
2 tablespoons red wine vinegar
1 pomegranate
1 handful mint leaves
1 handful flat-leaf (Italian) parsley
    leaves
1 small red onion, thinly sliced
    into half moons
Greek yoghurt, Middle Eastern flat
    bread and lettuce, to serve

Preheat a barbecue or grill (broiler) to very high. Cut the lamb into 3 cm (1¼ inch) chunks and season well with sea salt and freshly ground black pepper. Mix the harissa with the vinegar. Thread the lamb onto metal or soaked wooden skewers. Brush some of the harissa mixture on both sides of the lamb. Grill for 2 minutes each side.

Halve the pomegranate and bash the halves with a wooden spoon over a large bowl to catch all the seeds and the mess. Remove any white membrane from the seeds.

Serve the lamb with the herbs, pomegranate seeds, a dollop of the remaining harissa mixture, onion, yoghurt and crisp lettuce all wrapped up in the flat bread.

PREP AHEAD

The lamb can be marinated and refrigerated 1 day ahead.

THE SKINNY

Pastes such as harissa are an instant and skinny way to add flavour to meat or veg. Most supermarkets carry good-quality varieties. My favourite are the dark chunky mixes made with good-quality dried chillies.

Greek pork patties with tomato salad and radish tzatziki

preparation time 15 minutes / cooking time 10 minutes / serves 4

Fresh oregano is such a pungent herb and these grilled pork patties come alive with its woodsy taste. Garlicky tzatziki gains an edge with crisp chopped radishes swirled through. Serve with a fresh tomato salad or rice for the perfect summer or winter meal.

500 g (1 lb 2 oz) very lean minced (ground) pork
2 handfuls fresh soft breadcrumbs
1 small red onion, finely chopped
½ garlic clove, crushed or finely chopped
finely grated zest of 1 lemon
2 tablespoons oregano leaves, finely chopped
1 egg
cooking oil or spray

Radish tzatziki
200 g (7 oz/¾ cup) low-fat Greek yoghurt
1 tablespoon chopped dill
16 small radishes, roughly chopped or sliced
½ garlic clove, crushed or finely chopped
juice of ½ lemon

Mix together the pork, breadcrumbs, onion, garlic, lemon zest, oregano and egg and season with a good amount of sea salt and freshly ground black pepper. Mix well and form into 12 flat patties. Refrigerate until using.

To make the radish tzatziki, mix all the ingredients together and season.

Heat a barbecue, grill (broiler) or chargrill (griddle) pan to high. Rub the patties with a tiny bit of oil or spray and cook for 2–3 minutes each side. Serve with the tzatziki alongside.

PREP AHEAD

The patties can be made 1 day ahead and refrigerated. They freeze well, too — just thaw in the fridge on the day of using.

THE SKINNY

If you use extra-lean pork, these aren't too caloric. The fresh breadcrumbs soften them up so you don't need extra fat. Oil spray keeps the fat content down when cooking too.

Lamb steaks with parmesan pea purée

preparation time 15 minutes / cooking time 10 minutes / serves 4

Peas, mint and lamb are a dream trio. The flavours all dovetail together in perfect unison for a quick and simple mid-week meal. Edamame (soya beans) could also be used for an even healthier purée.

2 tablespoons balsamic vinegar
1 teaspoon extra virgin olive oil
2 garlic cloves, finely chopped
1 tablespoon wholegrain mustard
1 tablespoon honey
1 small handful mint leaves, chopped
4 lean lamb leg steaks (about 500 g/
   1 lb 2 oz), trimmed of all fat

Parmesan pea purée
500 g (1 lb 2 oz) frozen or fresh
   shelled peas
1 small handful mint leaves, chopped
4 spring onions (scallions), chopped
125 ml (4 fl oz/½ cup) vegetable
   or chicken stock
2 tablespoons grated parmesan

Mix the vinegar, olive oil, garlic, mustard, honey and mint together and season with sea salt and freshly ground black pepper. Coat the lamb steaks with the marinade and set aside.

To make the parmesan pea purée, blanch the peas in salted boiling water for 1–2 minutes. Drain, then purée in a food processor with the mint, spring onion, stock, parmesan and some salt. Pour into a saucepan to reheat.

Heat a barbecue, grill (broiler) or chargrill (griddle) pan to high. Cook the lamb steaks for about 2 minutes each side for medium. Allow to rest for 3 minutes, covered with foil, then serve with the pea purée.

PREP AHEAD

The lamb can be marinated 1 day ahead and refrigerated. Make the pea purée on the night of serving otherwise the colour will grey a bit.

THE SKINNY

Avoid lamb chops and cutlets, which have a lot more fat. Leg steaks are usually trimmed very lean but still have all the taste and tenderness of the other cuts. Lamb fillet is a good option too as it's very lean but it is a bit more expensive.

Pork and fennel tray roast with lemon and coriander paste

preparation time 10 minutes / cooking time 30 minutes / serves 4

Spice pastes are a clever way to bump up a tray of roasted vegetables and meat. Preserved lemon, smoky paprika and coriander are pureed together to make a sticky, citrus paste that is very special indeed.

2 large red-skinned potatoes, scrubbed, cut into 2.5 cm (1 inch) pieces
2 fennel bulbs, quartered and cores removed
3 red onions, quartered
2 pork fillets (about 350 g/12 oz each), halved lengthways and then widthways so you have 8 pieces
Greek yoghurt, to serve

Lemon and coriander paste
4 large preserved lemon quarters
1 garlic clove
½ thumb-sized red chilli, seeds removed
1 teaspoon smoked paprika
1 tablespoon honey
1 tablespoon chopped coriander (cilantro)
1 tablespoon olive oil
1 tablespoon water

Preheat the oven to 200°C (400°F/Gas 6). Drop the potato and fennel into a saucepan of lightly salted boiling water. Return to the boil, then cook for 1 minute. Drain well and spread out onto a tea towel-lined tray to dry.

To make the lemon and coriander paste, rinse the preserved lemon under running water, discard the flesh, saving the rind. Add to a food processor along with the remaining ingredients and process into a smooth purée.

Place all the vegetables and pork in a large roasting tray or two small ones. Rub the paste over the pork and a little bit on the veg as well. Season with sea salt and freshly ground black pepper and bake for 25 minutes or until the pork is cooked and the vegetables are golden. Serve with the yoghurt.

PREP AHEAD

The paste can be made 1 week ahead and refrigerated in an airtight container, drizzled with a little oil to keep it fresh.

THE SKINNY

Pastes such as this are wonderful because they create a sweet–sour glaze. Pork fillet is the leanest cut you can get, meltingly tender and fairly inexpensive.

Gaucho skirt steak with avocado and hearts of palm salad

preparation time 10 minutes / cooking time 10 minutes / serves 4

Dried Mexican chillies make incredible smoky rubs for meat. Toast them in a frying pan, then whiz them up in a spice grinder. It's worth this small amount of effort because home-ground chillies are so much fresher than bought ground mixes. Each variety of chilli has its own unique taste; ancho is very fruity while pasilla has a chocolate scent. If you don't have access to whole Mexican dried chillies, then use a good-quality chilli powder.

2 dried ancho or pasilla chillies
  (or 2 tablespoons pasilla or
  ancho chilli powder)
1 tablespoon smoked sweet paprika
1 teaspoon cocoa powder
600 g (1 lb 5 oz) skirt steak or
  4 lean eye-fillet or rump steaks
1 teaspoon olive oil
1 tablespoon caster (superfine) sugar

Salad

1 x 400 g (14 oz) tin hearts of palm,
  drained and sliced
1 large avocado, cut into chunky pieces
juice of 1 lime
10 cherry tomatoes, halved
1 small handful coriander (cilantro),
  chopped
1 teaspoon olive oil

Heat a non-stick frying pan over high heat until very hot. Toast the chillies for 30 seconds each side or until they puff up. Remove the stems and seeds. Roughly chop and place in a spice grinder with the smoked paprika and cocoa powder and process until ground. (The paprika will keep it dry and make it less sticky in the spice grinder.)

Rub the meat on both sides with the olive oil. Mix the sugar, about 1 teaspoon of sea salt and the ground chilli mixture together and sprinkle on both sides of the steaks.

To make the salad, mix all the ingredients together and season.

Heat a barbecue, grill (broiler) or chargrill (griddle) pan to high. Cook the steaks for 3 minutes each side for medium-rare. Rest for 5 minutes, covered. Serve sliced with the salad.

PREP AHEAD

The rub can be made a week ahead and stored in a screw-top jar to keep fresh. Make the salad just before eating to keep the colours vibrant.

THE SKINNY

A little bit of avocado is fine and goes well with red meat. Chilli rubs boost any type of grilled meat for almost no calories but enormous taste.

Sizzling Korean-style beef with sesame seeds

preparation time 15 minutes / cooking time 5 minutes / serves 4

Bulgogi, with its paper-thin slices of beef seared quickly with garlic and soy, is one of the best-known Korean dishes. The trick to making the beef ultra thin is to partially freeze it and then slice it. Rump steak when cut this way is very tender and, best of all, affordable.

500 g (1 lb 2 oz) beef rump steak
   or fillet, trimmed
3 tablespoons caster (superfine) sugar
3 tablespoons soy sauce
2 tablespoons mirin
2 garlic cloves, finely chopped
1 thumb-sized red chilli, seeds removed
   and sliced
1 teaspoon sesame oil
vegetable oil, for cooking
8 spring onions (scallions), cut into
   3 cm (1¼ inch) pieces
1 tablespoon sesame seeds, toasted
steamed rice, to serve

Thinly slice the beef. If you have any extra time, it helps if the meat is partially frozen, allowing you to slice it even thinner. Ten minutes in the freezer will help immensely. Combine the sugar, soy, mirin, garlic, chilli and sesame oil in a bowl. Add the beef and stir well to coat. Crack some black pepper over as well.

Heat a scant amount of vegetable oil in a wok over high heat until very hot. Cook half of the beef for 40 seconds, turning until browned, then remove from the wok and repeat with a little more oil and the remaining beef. Return all of the beef to the wok and add the spring onion. Stir-fry for 1 minute, then add the sesame seeds. Serve with the rice.

PREP AHEAD

Marinate the meat the night before and refrigerate it (or freeze it and simply thaw in the refrigerator on the day of cooking).

THE SKINNY

Soy and mirin are optimal skinny ingredients for stir-fries as they aren't caloric and add savoury taste.

Lamb with borlotti beans, basil oil and roasted cherry tomatoes

preparation time 10 minutes / cooking time 20 minutes / serves 4

My family and I put this combination together when we stayed near Nice, in France, one summer. Baskets of fresh pink-spotted borlotti beans were overflowing in the market and I was desperate to use them. They don't appear often so you have to act on it when you see them. At home I use tinned which are still very good.

300 g (10½ oz) cherry tomatoes
  on the vine
2 garlic cloves, finely chopped
3 tablespoons extra virgin olive oil
1 large handful basil leaves, chopped
4 tablespoons balsamic vinegar
2 x 400 g (14 oz) tins borlotti beans,
  drained and rinsed
500 g (1 lb 2 oz) lamb leg steaks,
  trimmed

Preheat the oven to 180°C (350°F/Gas 4). Place the tomatoes on a baking tray with half of the garlic and drizzle with 1 tablespoon of the olive oil. Roast for 15 minutes or until slightly collapsed.

Mix the basil and vinegar and remaining garlic and olive oil together and season with sea salt and freshly ground black pepper. Place the beans in a large frying pan and pour over three-quarters of the basil mixture. Gently cook over low heat until warmed through.

Preheat a barbecue, grill (broiler) or chargrill (griddle) pan to high. Rub the remaining basil mixture over the lamb and season. Cook for 2 minutes each side for medium-rare and serve with the beans and tomatoes.

PREP AHEAD

The basil mixture can be made a couple of hours ahead and the lamb marinated as well. Just before serving, prepare the tomatoes and warm beans and cook the lamb.

THE SKINNY

The sweet balsamic vinegar makes up for the need for excess oil in the herb dressing. Beans are satisfying, healthy and a quick base for salads or barbecued meats.

Steak with balsamic mushroom sauce and shoestring root vegetables

preparation time 20 minutes / cooking time 40 minutes / serves 4

Steak and mushroom is a classic. Add a reduction of balsamic vinegar to the sauce to make it even more lip-smacking. Scoop up the sauce with roasted root vegetables and serve a fresh green salad on the side. Try to use a balsamic that is mid-range in price, not the cheapest or the dearest but fairly good quality.

600 g (1 lb 5 oz) mixed root vegetables
(such as celeriac, carrot and
parsnips), peeled
olive oil spray
finely grated zest of 1 lemon
2 tablespoons olive oil
500 g (1 lb 2 oz) chestnut mushrooms,
trimmed and sliced
2 garlic cloves, finely chopped
4 tablespoons balsamic vinegar
2 tablespoons soft brown sugar
4 x 125 g (4½ oz) beef steaks (rump,
fillet or sirloin), trimmed of all fat
2 tablespoons finely chopped flat-leaf
(Italian) parsley

Preheat the oven to 190°C (375°F/Gas 5). Slice the vegetables into matchsticks, about 2 mm (1⁄16 inch) thick (a mandolin or food processor attachment is very handy for this). Place on two baking trays and spray with olive oil. Sprinkle over the lemon zest and season with sea salt and freshly ground black pepper. Roast for 40 minutes or until crisp.

Heat the olive oil in a large frying pan over high heat. Add the mushrooms and garlic along with a good pinch of salt. Cook for 5 minutes or until the mushrooms are browned. Mix the vinegar and sugar together and pour over the mushrooms. Stir to combine and cook for 1– 2 minutes or until the mixture becomes syrupy. Set aside.

Heat a barbecue, grill (broiler) or chargrill (griddle) pan to high. Season the steaks and cook for 2–3 minutes each side, depending on the thickness of the steaks, for medium-rare. Rest for 5 minutes, then reheat the mushroom sauce, adding any resting juices from the meat. Serve with the crisp vegetables and a sprinkle of parsley over everything.

PREP AHEAD

The mushroom sauce can be made a couple of hours before and then reheated. The vegetables can be sliced 4 hours ahead and kept in cold water. Drain well on a tea towel before baking.

THE SKINNY

Steak is assumed to be fattening but it doesn't have to be. Buy lean cuts, such as rump or fillet, and trim off excess fat. Balsamic vinegar is a faultless skinny ingredient in sauces that normally use butter or cream.

Beef and pea keema curry

preparation time 10 minutes / cooking time 30 minutes / serves 4

My Indian friend Rita gave me this recipe. Her family calles it 'hamburger curry' because it uses ground beef. Keema translates as 'minced' and it's considered the nursery food of India. Children, though, aren't the only ones to find it comforting and tasty. It's pretty mild in heat and spice, so if you want it hotter, just throw in some chilli flakes. I like to use standard curry powder that's typically bright yellow in colour. Be sure to use a fresh fragrant one. Spices lose their punch after six to eight months so check your spice cupboard first.

2 teaspoons vegetable oil
500 g (1 lb 2 oz) lean minced (ground) beef
1 large onion, finely chopped
2 garlic cloves, chopped
1 tablespoon finely chopped ginger
1 large floury potato, cut into 3 cm (1¼ inch) dice
2 carrots, cut into 3 cm (1¼ inch) dice
2 tablespoons mild curry powder
1 tablespoon tomato paste (concentrated purée)
500 ml (17 fl oz/2 cups) beef or vegetable stock
60 g (2¼ oz) frozen or fresh shelled peas
steamed basmati rice, coriander (cilantro) leaves and mango or lime chutney, to serve

Heat 1 teaspoon of the vegetable oil in a frying pan over high heat. Add the beef and cook for about 5 minutes or until crisp and golden, breaking up any lumps with the back of a wooden spoon. Remove from the pan, discarding the fat, and set aside.

Wipe out the pan and heat the remaining oil. Add the onion, garlic and ginger and season with sea salt and freshly ground black pepper. Cook for 8 minutes or until softened. Add the potato, carrot and curry powder and cook for another couple of minutes. Add the tomato paste, stock and minced beef and stir together. Reduce the heat to medium and cook for 15 minutes. During the last 5 minutes, add the peas. Serve with the basmati rice, coriander leaves and mango or lime chutney.

PREP AHEAD

The curry can be made 1–2 days ahead and refrigerated or frozen. Gently reheat, adding a little extra stock or water as it will have thickened up.

THE SKINNY

Usually minced meat is fattening but if you buy lean minced steak, it can still be healthy. With three types of vegetables included, this is a one-pot healthy meal.

Mirin and soy-poached beef and onion stew

preparation time 15 minutes / cooking time 10 minutes / serves 4

This unusually prepared Japanese dish is called oyakodon. The beef is quickly poached in a tasty mirin and soy stock and served over rice. Traditionally a beaten egg is poured into the poaching liquid to thicken it. I have left this out to keep it slimmer but it's an option you can choose.

500 g (1 lb 2 oz) rump steak
300 ml (10½ fl oz) vegetable stock
100 ml (3½ fl oz) soy sauce
200 ml (7 fl oz) mirin
2 tablespoons caster (superfine) sugar
2 brown onions, thinly sliced
  into half moons
1 tablespoon pickled ginger, chopped
6 spring onions (scallions), finely
  chopped
1 thumb-sized red chilli, seeds removed
  and thinly sliced
steamed rice, to serve

Place the beef in the freezer while you prepare the other ingredients. Combine the stock, soy, mirin and sugar in a saucepan, bring to the boil, then reduce the heat to a simmer. Add the onion and cook for 5 minutes.

Thinly slice the beef, add to the pan, then remove from the heat. Divide the soup among bowls and sprinkle with the pickled ginger, spring onion and chilli. Serve with the rice.

PREP AHEAD

The meat can be sliced and poaching liquid prepared up to 8 hours ahead.

THE SKINNY

Poaching is a slim method to cook meat, keeping it juicy without using fat. The soy and mirin provide a delicious sauce, so you won't feel like you're missing out on anything.

Pork scallopine with lemon-wine sauce

preparation time 20 minutes / cooking time 25 minutes / serves 4

Traditionally this would be done with veal, which is both expensive and not very politically correct to eat, but pork fillet makes a shoo-in substitute and is equally tender.

400 g (14 oz) pork fillet
plain (all-purpose) flour, for dusting
1 tablespoon olive oil
3 small French shallots (eschalots),
  finely chopped
juice of 1 lemon
200 ml (7 fl oz) chicken stock
200 ml (7 fl oz) white wine
1 tablespoon baby capers in brine,
  drained
2 tablespoons flat-leaf (Italian) parsley,
  finely chopped
cooked Puy (tiny blue-green) lentils,
  crushed boiled new potatoes
  or blanched broccoli, to serve

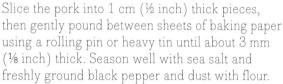

Slice the pork into 1 cm (½ inch) thick pieces, then gently pound between sheets of baking paper using a rolling pin or heavy tin until about 3 mm (⅛ inch) thick. Season well with sea salt and freshly ground black pepper and dust with flour.

Heat a large non-stick frying pan over high heat until very hot. Heat 1 teaspoon of the olive oil, add one-quarter of the pork fillets and cook for 1–2 minutes each side or until browned. Remove from the pan and repeat with the remaining pork and olive oil. It's important to keep the pan really hot or the pork will stick and need more oil. Remove from the pan.

Add the shallot to the pan with some seasoning and cook until soft. Add the lemon juice, stock and wine and cook for 5 minutes or until reduced by half. Return the meat to the pan along with the capers and cook for 30 seconds or until just heated through. Scatter with chopped parsley and serve with lentils, potatoes or broccoli if you like.

PREP AHEAD

The pork can be sliced and pounded 1 day ahead and refrigerated, stored between sheets of baking paper.

THE SKINNY

Lemon, capers and wine create a tasty sauce without the need for cream or butter. Pork fillet cooks quickly and is very low in fat.

No-cream Swedish meatballs with dill

preparation time 15 minutes / cooking time 20 minutes / serves 4

Everyone adores meatballs. They're the perfect comfort food. They're just fun to eat, plain and simple. Swedish food is one of my favourite cuisines but with the cream added to most dishes, it's a bit fattening. Reduced beef stock and dill create a tasty sauce here.

500 g (1 lb 2 oz) lean minced
   (ground) pork
2 teaspoons ground allspice
1 egg
1 small onion, finely diced
75 g (2⅔ oz) fresh white breadcrumbs
1 tablespoon olive oil
1 tablespoon plain (all-purpose) flour
125 ml (4 fl oz/½ cup) white wine
400 ml (14 fl oz) beef stock
3 teaspoons finely chopped dill
jarred cranberry sauce, to serve
boiled green vegetables or potatoes,
   to serve (optional)

Preheat the oven to 190°C (375°F/Gas 5). Combine the pork with the allspice, egg, onion and breadcrumbs in a bowl and season with sea salt and freshly ground black pepper. Mix well and form into golf-ball-sized meatballs. Place on a large baking tray, toss with a bit of the olive oil and season. Bake for 15 minutes or until browned. You won't need to turn them. When you remove them, use a metal spatula to scrape them from the tray.

Heat the remaining olive oil in a non-stick frying pan over medium–low heat. Add the flour and cook for 2 minutes or until lightly browned, then add the wine and stock. Whisk until it is a thick sauce. Add the meatballs to the pan and cook for 2–3 minutes or until well coated. Scatter over the dill and serve with the cranberry sauce and vegetables or potatoes.

PREP AHEAD

The meatballs can be rolled 1 day ahead and refrigerated or frozen. They can be baked and frozen as well.

THE SKINNY

Baking meatballs requires far less oil than pan-frying. The fresh dill lifts the sauce and compensates for the lack of cream.

Stir-frying: the definitive guide

This genius method of cooking is quick, healthy and makes the perfect one-pot meal with rice or noodles. Mix and match your ingredients for a delicious lunch or dinner.

EQUIPMENT You will need a large wok and two long wooden spoons to cook with. Asian supermarkets are the best places to buy them and they are inexpensive. The best type of wok is carbon steel.

To season a new wok, place it over high heat until nearly smoking. Dip some paper towel in vegetable oil and wipe the surface of the wok — use tongs as it will be very hot. Place the wok back over low heat and heat for 10 minutes. Remove and allow to cool. Rinse with water (never detergent) and wipe the surface with a bit more oil. It's now ready to use.

Whenver you are stir-frying, always heat the wok until smoking hot, then add your oil.

After using, always wipe with oil to prevent rust from forming.

COMBINATIONS Try to choose one protein and one to three vegetables. One of the vegetables should be crisp, like capsicum or broccoli, so there is a contrast in textures. Too many ingredients isn't good either — less is more!

PREPARATION Before you start to cook, it's important to have everything ready to go. The cooking time is short so chop all the ingredients, make the sauce and cook the rice before stir-frying.

THE ESSENTIAL FLAVOUR BASE This is the base for any of the suggested sauces. It is wok-fried just before the vegetables are added:

- 1 thumb-sized red chilli, seeds removed and sliced
- 2 garlic cloves, sliced
- 4 cm (1½ inch) piece of ginger, shredded

COMPONENTS It's as easy as choosing your protein, two to four types of vegetables and then your sauce.

<u>Protein</u> To serve four people, 500 g (1 1b 2 oz) of meat or seafood is a good guide. If using tofu, then reduce the quantity to 400 g (14 oz). If you like, to add more flavour and give a crisp edge to your protein, mix your meat, seafood or tofu with 1 teaspoon of soy sauce and 1 tablespoon of cornflour (cornstarch). The following proteins are ideal for stir-frying.

- turkey fillets, cut into 3 cm (1¼ inch) thick slices
- chicken (thigh or breast) fillets, cut into 3 cm (1¼ inch) thick slices
- beef or pork, cut into 3 cm (1¼ inch) thick slices, or use lean minced (ground) meat
- sliced squid
- whole peeled raw prawns
- 400 g (14 oz) drained and pressed firm tofu, cut into 3 cm (1¼ inch) cubes

<u>Vegetables, crunch and noodles</u> As with protein, 500 g (1 lb 2 oz) of vegetables or a mixture of noodles and veg is a good amount to feed four people. Choose one to four components for a well-balanced mix. For the vegetables, slice each into 3 cm (1¼ inch) pieces so they cook at the same time. These are some of my favourite vegetable and noodle additions to stir-fries.

- red or white onions or spring onions (scallions)
- red or yellow capsicum (peppers)
- broccoli
- green or snake (yard-long) beans
- Chinese greens like Chinese broccoli (gai larn), choy sum or bok choy
- cherry tomatoes
- chunks of pineapple
- bean sprouts
- savoy or Chinese cabbage
- kale
- carrot

- celery
- sugar snap peas or snow peas (mangetout)
- baby corn
- toasted cashews or roasted peanuts
- shiitake mushrooms or quartered button mushrooms
- water chestnuts or bamboo shoots
- noodles: soaked rice noodles, ramen, udon, somen, buckwheat, Chinese egg or fresh egg noodles

<u>Sauces</u> Use these sauce mixtures in addition to the essential flavour base (see opposite) with your choice of protein, vegetables and/or noodles. Each sauce makes about 200 ml (7 fl oz), which is a generous amount so that you have a little extra to dribble on rice. Dark soy is preferable to regular soy sauce. It's aged with molasses and thickened with cornflour (cornstarch), which results in a more full-bodied liquid that has much less salt.

· ·

Oyster or hoisin sauce (and black bean sauce)

Red meats like pork combined with greens, such as Chinese broccoli (gai larn), baby corn, red onion and water chestnuts are lovely with this.

2 tablespoons chicken stock
  or Shaoxing rice wine
2 tablespoons oyster or hoisin sauce
1 tablespoon soft brown sugar

1 tablespoon lime juice
2 teaspoons dark or regular soy sauce
1 teaspoon cornflour (cornstarch),
  dissolved in 2 teaspoons water

Mix all the ingredients in a small bowl.

NOTE For a black bean sauce version, add 1 tablespoon salted black beans and 1 chopped garlic clove to the mixture.

· ·

Spicy Chinese Sichuan sauce

Chicken breast, broccoli, red onion and toasted cashews pair nicely with this sauce.

2 tablespoons chicken stock
2 tablespoons dark or regular soy sauce
1 tablespoon Chinese black vinegar
1 tablespoon Shaoxing rice wine

2 teaspoons chilli bean sauce
2 teaspoons cornflour (cornstarch),
    dissolved in 1 tablespoon water
1 teaspoon caster (superfine) sugar

Mix all the ingredients in a small bowl and stir until the sugar has dissolved.

NOTE If you can't find Chinese black vinegar, use normal red vinegar. For a rice wine substitute, use dry sherry, and you can use any type of chilli sauce or paste if you can't find the chilli bean sauce.

Sweet and sour chilli sauce

Especially notable with beef, green beans, julienned carrots and rice noodles.

2 tablespoons dark or regular soy sauce
2 tablespoons lime juice

75 ml (2⅛ fl oz) sweet chilli dipping sauce
2 teaspoons fish sauce

Mix all the ingredients in a small bowl.

Chinese lemon sauce

My best-loved combination with chicken breast, spring onions and broccoli.

3 tablespoons chicken stock
3 tablespoons honey
1 tablespoon soy sauce

2 teaspoons cornflour (cornstarch),
    dissolved in 1 tablespoon water
½ teaspoon Chinese five-spice
finely grated zest and juice of 2 lemons

Mix all the ingredients in a small bowl.

South-East Asian lime and basil sauce

Chicken thighs, green beans, cherry tomatoes, fresh pineapple and red onion are my favourite combination to use with this sweet and sour sauce.

juice of 2 limes
3 tablespoons chicken stock
1 tablespoon fish sauce

1 tablespoon soft brown sugar
1 tablespoon very finely chopped lemongrass
1 large handful Thai or regular basil leaves

Mix the lime juice, stock, fish sauce, sugar and lemongrass in a bowl. Add the basil leaves to the stir-fry at the very end of the cooking time.

NOTE This makes less liquid than the other sauces but this type of Thai/Vietnamese stir-fry doesn't use as much.

Japanese soy, mirin and honey sauce

Foolproof with beef, shiitake mushrooms, spring onions and noodles.

3 tablespoons mirin
2 tablespoons lime juice
2 tablespoons Japanese soy sauce

1 tablespoon honey
2 teaspoons cornflour (cornstarch),
  dissolved in 1 tablespoon water

Mix all the ingredients in a small bowl.

Tamarind-glazed chicken with green chilli, mint and tomato salad

preparation time 15 minutes / cooking time 10 minutes / serves 4

A sweet and sour tamarind glaze turns these chicken skewers into something special. Although you can just grill the chicken breasts with the sauce, it's much nicer on a skewer because you get more of the sticky sauce.

100 g (3½ oz) jarred tamarind purée
1 tablespoon finely grated ginger
2 teaspoons mild chilli powder
2 teaspoons black or yellow mustard seeds
2 tablespoons honey
4 skinless chicken breast fillets, cut into chunky 3 cm (1¼ inch) pieces
cooked basmati rice and low-fat Greek yoghurt, to serve

Salad
250 g (9 oz) cherry tomatoes, halved
1 small red onion, sliced into half moons
1 small handful mint leaves, chopped
2 tablespoons chopped coriander (cilantro)
1 thumb-sized green chilli, seeds removed and thinly sliced
pinch of mild chilli powder
pinch of black or yellow mustard seeds
juice of ½ lemon

Combine the tamarind, ginger, chilli powder, mustard seeds and honey in a small bowl and season with sea salt and freshly ground black pepper. Soak some wooden skewers or use metal ones. Thread the meat onto the skewers, brush with some of the marinade and set aside until cooking (see Note).

To make the salad, mix all the ingredients together and season.

Preheat a barbecue or grill (broiler) to high. Cook the chicken skewers for 2 minutes each side. Remove, brush heavily with the glaze and cook for another minute or until cooked through.

Serve with the salad, rice, remaining marinade and yoghurt.

NOTE Be sure you set some marinade aside for serving to avoid cross-contamination with the raw chicken from the brush.

PREP AHEAD

The chicken can be marinated and threaded onto skewers 8 hours ahead. You can also freeze it this way and thaw it in the refrigerator on the day of cooking.

THE SKINNY

Tamarind purée is a zero calorie/fat ingredient that adds bags of flavour and doubles as a glaze.

Turkish chicken escalopes with yoghurt marinade

preparation time 15 minutes / cooking time 10 minutes / serves 4

Yoghurt not only tenderises meat, it also makes an exceptional marinade. Flattening the chicken breasts may seem like an extra step but it makes them fork tender and decreases the cooking time. This is also very good with Turkish salsa (see page 20).

4 skinless chicken breasts fillets
juice of 1 lemon
1 garlic clove, crushed
200 g (7 oz/¾ cup) low-fat Greek
    yoghurt
1 small onion, grated
1 teaspoon ground cumin
1 teaspoon ground coriander
1 teaspoon hot paprika
2 tablespoons chopped mint,
    plus extra leaves to serve
1 teaspoon olive oil
steamed basmati rice or a green salad,
    to serve

Slice each chicken breast lengthways so that you have two flat pieces. Place each piece between sheets of baking paper and pound to about 1.5 cm (⅝ inch) with a rolling pin or meat mallet. Place in a glass dish or bowl and season well with sea salt and freshly ground black pepper. Add the lemon juice, garlic, yoghurt, onion, spices and mint in a bowl. Mix well and refrigerate until using.

Preheat a barbecue or grill (broiler) to high. Season and drizzle the chicken with olive oil to keep it from sticking. Cook for about 3 minutes each side or until just cooked through.

Sprinkle the chicken with the extra mint leaves. Serve with rice or a crisp green salad.

PREP AHEAD

The chicken can be marinated 1 day ahead and even frozen in the marinade.

THE SKINNY

Yoghurt is a tremendous skinny ingredient for so many reasons. It can work as a marinade, dressing, instant sauce or it can be dolloped on a dish to finish instead of cream. Any spices, fresh herbs or jarred curry pastes are wonderful mixed with it as well.

Stuffed chicken breasts with spinach, cinnamon and dates

preparation time 10 minutes / cooking time 35 minutes / serves 4

This one-dish chicken dinner is stuffed with sweet caramelised onion, spinach and sticky dates and baked with sour pomegranate molasses. It's a wholesome combination and full of tantalising tastes of the Middle East.

2 large onions, thinly sliced

2 garlic cloves, sliced

1 tablespoon olive oil

2 teaspoons ground cumin

4 large soft dates, pitted and chopped

200 g (7 oz) baby spinach

4 skinless chicken breast fillets

1 teaspoon ground cinnamon

3 tablespoons pomegranate molasses
    or honey

steamed couscous or burghul (bulgur)
    tossed with lemon juice and
    chopped parsley, to serve

Preheat the oven to 200°C (400°F/Gas 6).

In a large non-stick frying pan over medium heat, sauté the onion and garlic with a splash of olive oil and some sea salt and freshly ground black pepper for 10 minutes or until golden. Add the cumin, dates, spinach and a bit more seasoning and cook for another minute or two or until the spinach has wilted. Remove from the heat and cool.

Cut the chicken breasts lengthways without cutting all the way through so they open up like a book. Divide the stuffing between the breasts, fold the breasts back over and place in a shallow baking dish. Rub the cinnamon over the breasts and season. Drizzle over the pomegranate molasses and bake for 20 minutes or until just cooked through. Serve with the couscous.

PREP AHEAD

The breasts can be stuffed 1 day ahead and baked just before serving. They can also be frozen and thawed in the fridge on the day of using.

THE SKINNY

Dates are an excellent skinny ingredient, lending sweetness to savoury food. The pomegranate molasses works as a zero calorie sauce as it's made from only reduced juices.

Tostadas with spicy tomato turkey

preparation time 10 minutes / cooking time 20 minutes / serves 4

Ground turkey is a star ingredient as it's inexpensive, has practically nil fat and cooks up a pearly white colour. Here it's pan-fried with a spicy, tangy tomato sauce and served up on a crisp baked corn tortilla. You can also use flour wraps, which are even lower in fat.

8 fresh corn tortillas
1 teaspoon olive oil, plus extra
   for brushing
1 onion, finely chopped
2 garlic cloves, chopped
500 g (1 lb 2 oz) minced (ground)
   turkey
3 teaspoons ground cumin
3 teaspoons smoked paprika
2 tablespoons soft brown sugar
75 ml (2⅜ fl oz) apple cider vinegar
300 ml (10½ fl oz) tomato passata
   (puréed tomatoes) or tinned
   chopped tomatoes
1 avocado, chopped into chunks
1 small red onion, finely chopped
1 large handful coriander (cilantro),
   chopped

Preheat the oven to 200°C (400°F/Gas 6). Brush the tortillas on both sides with olive oil. Place in a single layer on a baking tray and bake for 7–8 minutes or until crisp and golden. Remove and set aside.

Meanwhile, heat the olive oil in a large frying pan over medium–high heat. Sauté the onion and garlic with some sea salt and freshly ground black pepper for about 5 minutes or until the onion has softened. Add the turkey and cook, breaking up the meat with the back of a spoon, for about 4 minutes or until thoroughly browned. Add the cumin, paprika, sugar, vinegar and tomato passata and cook for another 10 minutes or until most of the liquid has evaporated.

Spoon the meat over the tostadas and top with the avocado, onion and coriander.

PREP AHEAD

The turkey mixture can be made 1–2 days ahead and refrigerated. It can also be frozen and thawed in the fridge on the day of using.

THE SKINNY

Although you can use soft flour tortillas, it's just not the same as crunching into a crisp one. Brushing and baking is a clever way to replace deep-frying. Minced turkey is very lean but can cook up dry so the tomato passata keeps it juicy.

Crisp mustard and tarragon chicken with roasted cherry tomatoes

preparation time 10 minutes / cooking time 30 minutes / serves 4

Toasted breadcrumbs are pressed into mustard-tarragon-rubbed chicken breasts and baked until crisp in this cheat's version of fried chicken. The roasted cherry tomatoes provide a tasty sauce to serve alongside.

4 skinless chicken breast fillets,
   tenderloins removed
2 tablespoons Dijon mustard
2 French shallots (eschalots),
   finely chopped
2 tablespoons chopped tarragon leaves,
   plus whole leaves for garnishing
150 g (5½ oz) fresh fine breadcrumbs,
   toasted until golden
2 tablespoons olive oil or olive oil spray
250 g (9 oz) cherry tomatoes
2 garlic cloves, thickly sliced
boiled baby (new) potatoes, to serve

Preheat the oven to 200°C (400°F/Gas 6). Pound the breasts a little to flatten. Sprinkle the chicken with sea salt and freshly ground black pepper. Mix the mustard, tarragon and shallot together and spread all over the chicken. Roll in the breadcrumbs and place on a baking tray. Drizzle or spray both sides of the chicken with a little of the olive oil. Bake for 30 minutes or until crisp and brown.

Place the tomatoes and garlic in a small baking dish. Drizzle over the remaining olive oil and season, then place in the oven after the chicken has been cooking for 15 minutes. Serve the chicken with the tomatoes and potatoes and garnish with the tarragon.

PREP AHEAD

The chicken can be coated 1 day ahead and refrigerated or frozen. Thaw in the fridge on the day of using.

THE SKINNY

Mustard is a zero calorie way to add depth but no fat. It also gives the breadcrumbs something to stick to so you don't have to go to the trouble of dipping in flour, egg and all of that business.

Chicken, cherry and pistachio pilaf

preparation time 10 minutes / cooking time 35 minutes / serves 4

Traditional pilafs and biryanis take a fair amount of skill and time to get right and are usually made with chunks of lamb. This modern interpretation with aromatic allspice and sweet dried cherries uses quick-cooking chicken breast for a speedy weeknight supper. Serve with Greek yoghurt.

275 g (9¾ oz) basmati rice
1 tablespoon olive oil
2 large onions, thinly sliced
4 skinlesss chicken breast fillets,
    cut into 2 cm (¾ inch) pieces
3 tablespoons dried cherries,
    roughly chopped
1 teaspoon ground allspice
1 cinnamon stick
500 ml (17 fl oz/2 cups) chicken stock
2 tablespoons finely chopped flat-leaf
    (Italian) parsley
2 tablespoons pistachios, chopped
low-fat Greek yoghurt, to serve

Rinse the rice three or four times until the water runs clear. Drain and set aside. Heat the olive oil in a large heavy saucepan over medium heat. Add the onion and season with sea salt and freshly ground black pepper. Sauté for 12–15 minutes or until very golden and crisp at the edges. Add the chicken, cherries, allspice and cinnamon and sauté for 2 minutes or until opaque. Add the rice and stock and bring to the boil. Reduce the heat and simmer, covered with a lid, for 15 minutes. The liquid should be all absorbed. Stir the parsley through, scatter with the pistachios and serve with the yoghurt.

PREP AHEAD

The pilaf is best made just before serving.

THE SKINNY

All of the components in this rice dish are virtuous with the exception of the olive oil and pistachios. However, only small amounts of these are used but the taste still comes through.

Chicken with celery salt rub and cider-mustard slaw

preparation time 15 minutes / cooking time 10 minutes / serves 4

Adaptable for both summer and winter eating, the grilled chicken and mustardy cabbage slaw works in either season. Celery salt, a spice that isn't featured often, makes a particularly good rub for chicken or seafood.

4 skinless chicken breast fillets
2 teaspoons celery salt
1 teaspoon mild chilli powder, or to taste
1 teaspoon olive oil

Cider-mustard slaw
2 tablespoons apple cider vinegar
2 tablespoons wholegrain mustard
1 tablespoon honey
35 ml (1 fl oz) olive oil
¼ purple cabbage (about 500 g/
   1 lb 2 oz), finely shredded
2 carrots, finely shredded
1 granny smith apple, core removed
   and chopped into matchsticks
1 small white onion, finely chopped

Using a meat mallet, gently pound the chicken breasts so they are an even thickness all over. Mix the spices together with some sea salt and freshly ground black pepper. Rub the olive oil into the chicken, then sprinkle the spices over. Preheat a barbecue, grill (broiler) or chargrill (griddle) pan to high.

To make the cider-mustard slaw, mix together the vinegar, mustard, honey and olive oil in a small bowl and season. Place the cabbage, carrot, apple and onion in a large bowl. Pour the dressing over and mix.

Cook the chicken for 4–5 minutes each side and serve with the slaw.

PREP AHEAD

The chicken can be coated and refrigerated 1 day ahead or frozen. Thaw in the fridge on the day of using. The slaw can be made 3 hours before and refrigerated.

THE SKINNY

Spice rubs add dimension to grilled meats without the fat. Honey, vinegar and mustard make a tasty dressing with very little oil.

Jamaican chicken curry

preparation time 10 minutes / cooking time 25 minutes / serves 4

This Caribbean dish is lavished with green chillis, ginger and allspice, a trademark trio of Jamaican flavours. The cherry tomatoes and sweet potato add colour and extra veg to this aromatic curry.

2 teaspoons olive oil
1 large onion, chopped
5 cm (2 inch) piece of ginger, chopped
1 thumb-sized green chilli, finely
    chopped
2 garlic cloves, chopped
1 tablespoon curry powder
½ teaspoon ground allspice
½ teaspoon sweet paprika
2 cinnamon sticks
1 large sweet potato (kumara), peeled
    and cut into 3 cm (1¼ inch) chunks
4 skinless chicken breast fillets, chopped
    into 3 cm (1¼ inch) chunks
500 ml (17 fl oz/2 cups) chicken stock
1 tablespoon white wine vinegar
100 g (3½ oz) cherry tomatoes
coriander (cilantro) leaves and steamed
    basmati rice, to serve

Heat the olive oil in a large frying pan over medium heat and sauté the onion, ginger, chilli and garlic for 5 minutes or until soft. Season with sea salt and freshly ground black pepper and add the spices. Sauté for another minute, then add the sweet potato and chicken. Pour in the stock and vinegar. Cook for 15 minutes or until the sweet potato is cooked through. During the last 5 minutes of cooking, add the tomatoes. Scatter with the coriander and serve with the rice.

PREP AHEAD

The curry can be made 1 day ahead but undercook the sweet potatoes or they will go mushy when reheated. This curry freezes well.

THE SKINNY

Spices, chillies and ginger make this anything but boring. Stock is used instead of coconut milk, which is less caloric.

Chicken, ginger and green bean hotpot

preparation time 10 minutes / cooking time 20 minutes / serves 4

The ginger quantity sounds large here in this classic Vietnamese braise but it sweetens when cooking and doesn't overpower the dish at all. The Vietnamese add a little sugar to their stir-fries or stews to impart a caramel flavour. When combined with the fish sauce, poached ginger and stock, it's a captivating sauce.

1 tablespoon vegetable oil
5 cm (2 inch) piece of ginger,
    cut into julienne
2 garlic cloves, chopped
1 onion, thinly sliced into half moons
2 tablespoons fish sauce
1 tablespoon soft brown sugar
500 g (1 lb 2 oz) skinless chicken thigh
    fillets, trimmed of all fat and cut in half
250 ml (9 fl oz/1 cup) chicken stock
100 g (3½ oz) green beans, cut into
    2.5 cm (1 inch) lengths
2 tablespoons chopped coriander
    (cilantro)
steamed rice, to serve

Heat the vegetable oil in a saucepan over medium–high heat. Add the ginger, garlic and onion and stir-fry for about 5 minutes or until lightly golden. Add the fish sauce, sugar, chicken and stock. Cover and cook over medium heat for 15 minutes. In the last 2 minutes of cooking, add the green beans. Remove from the heat and stir through half of the coriander. Serve with the rice and the remaining coriander scattered over.

PREP AHEAD

The hotpot can be made 1 day ahead and refrigerated or frozen.

THE SKINNY

The large amounts of ginger and fish sauce infuse the sauce with flavour and make for a very lean dish with little oil.

Italian chicken braise with mushrooms and tomatoes

preparation time 15 minutes / cooking time 35 minutes / serves 4

Dried porcini, once soaked, produce an intense woodsy stock as well as being delicious mushrooms. Both are used in this quick Italian chicken stew for a wonderful rich intensity. Chicken breasts can be used instead, and would make it even lower in fat, but they are not quite as tender as the thighs.

250 ml (9 fl oz/1 cup) boiling water

25 g (1 oz) dried porcini mushrooms

2 tablespoons olive oil

6 skinless chicken thigh fillets, trimmed of all fat, cut into bite-sized pieces

1 large brown onion, thinly sliced into half moons

2 slices prosciutto, chopped

4 garlic cloves, chopped

200 g (7 oz) chestnut mushrooms, quartered

1 x 400 g (14 oz) tin whole roma (plum) tomatoes

125 ml (4 fl oz/½ cup) dry white wine

chopped flat-leaf (Italian) parsley and steamed rice or crushed boiled baby (new) potatoes, to serve

Pour the boiling water over the porcini mushrooms. Allow to soak for 10 minutes, then drain the liquid into a cup and save for later. Rinse and chop the mushrooms and set aside. Heat a little of the olive oil in a saucepan over medium–high heat. Season the chicken with sea salt and freshly ground black pepper and brown on all sides, about 4 minutes. Remove from the pan and add the onion, prosciutto, garlic and remaining olive oil and some seasoning. Sauté for 8 minutes or until the onion is golden, then add the chestnut mushrooms, porcini mushrooms and tomatoes and sauté for 5 minutes. Add the chicken, wine and reserved porcini soaking liquid. Cover and cook over medium–low heat for 15 minutes or until the chicken is tender. Check the seasoning. Add some parsley and serve with rice or crushed potatoes.

PREP AHEAD

The braise can be made 2 days ahead and refrigerated or frozen — simply thaw in the fridge on the day of using.

THE SKINNY

Dried mushrooms and the soaking liquid add flavour to stews without the need for cream. The prosciutto is used in small quantities but still adds a hint of saltiness.

Chicken baked with figs, honey and almonds

preparation time 5 minutes / cooking time 20 minutes / serves 4

When I see fat ripe purple figs in season I like to devise something with them while at their juicy peak. This was a simple Moorish-inspired dish I threw together one evening. The figs break down slightly when cooking, making a jammy sauce for the chicken. It can be made from start to finish in 25 minutes.

1 tablespoon olive oil
2 garlic cloves, sliced
2 tablespoons sherry vinegar
1 tablespoon honey
1 teaspoon ground cinnamon
2 tablespoons flaked almonds, toasted
4 skinless chicken breasts fillets
6 ripe purple figs, quartered
2 tablespoons finely chopped flat-leaf
   (Italian) parsley
steamed couscous, steamed green beans
   and low-fat Greek yoghurt, to serve

Preheat the oven to 190°C (375°F/Gas 5). Combine the olive oil, garlic, vinegar, honey, cinnamon and almonds in a bowl and season well. Add the chicken and toss to coat. Transfer to a roasting tray, scatter with the figs and bake for 20 minutes or until the chicken is just cooked through. Scatter over the parsley and serve with the couscous, green beans and yoghurt.

PREP AHEAD

The dish can be prepared 4–6 hours ahead and refrigerated, then baked shortly before serving.

THE SKINNY

Roasting or stewing fruit with savoury food is a healthy, winning duo. Toasted almonds add crunch and as only a small quantity is used fat is not a worry.

Ramen noodles with minced turkey, green beans and hoisin sauce

preparation time 10 minutes / cooking time 10 minutes / serves 4

Ground meat suits noodle stir-fries because they absorb more of the tastes and tuck into the noodles easily. Chilli bean paste, a Chinese condiment, is made with fermented soya beans, chilli and garlic. It's fiery but has a wonderful addictive taste. A little dollop into a stir-fry adds a 'umami' factor. Most supermarkets sell it in the international section. Failing that, you can buy it at an Asian food store, and one jar will last more than a year. Other Asian chilli pastes will also substitute well.

150 ml (5 fl oz) hoisin sauce
juice of 2 limes
2 tablespoons chilli bean paste
   or Chinese chilli sauce
1 tablespoon vegetable oil
500 g (1 lb 2 oz) minced (ground)
   turkey
3 garlic cloves, chopped
150 g (5½ oz) green beans, trimmed
   and halved
6 spring onions (scallions), chopped
200 g (7 oz) dried ramen noodles,
   to serve

Bring a large saucepan of salted water to the boil while you get everything ready.

Mix together the hoisin, lime juice and chilli sauce in a small bowl. Heat half of the vegetable oil in a wok over high heat, add the turkey and stir-fry, breaking up any lumps with the back of a wooden spoon, until nicely browned. Remove from the wok.

Add the remaining oil to the wok along with the garlic and cook until just golden. Add the beans and spring onion. Drop the noodles into the boiling water and cook for 3–4 minutes. Keep stir-frying the vegetables for 1 minute, then add the turkey and hoisin mixture. Stir-fry for 2–3 minutes or until the meat is warmed through and the sauce is sticky. Drain the noodles and serve in bowls with the turkey mixture spooned over.

PREP AHEAD

The sauce and vegetables can be chopped a couple of hours ahead and everything stir-fried just before eating.

THE SKINNY

Chinese condiments like hoisin and chilli bean paste add a salty-chilli spike to the plain turkey but have little fat.

Veggie

Thai pumpkin curry with pineapple, beans and tomatoes

preparation time 15 minutes / cooking time 15 minutes / serves 4

Thai red curry paste is a godsend for quick weekday cooking. Butternut pumpkin is a stalwart vegetarian ingredient and especially good in curries. Fresh sweet pineapple and cherry tomatoes elevate this further for a spectacular Thai dinner.

1 tablespoon vegetable oil

3 tablespoons red curry paste

1 x 400 ml (14 fl oz) tin low-fat
  coconut milk

250 g (9 oz) butternut pumpkin
  (winter squash), peeled and
  cut into 3 cm (1¼ inch) chunks

1 tablespoon fish sauce

finely grated zest and juice of 2 limes

100 g (3½ oz) green beans, trimmed
  and halved

100 g (3½ oz) cherry tomatoes

½ small pineapple, peeled, cored
  and cut into 3 cm (1¼ inch) pieces

coriander (cilantro) leaves and
  steamed rice, to serve

Heat the vegetable oil in a saucepan over medium–high heat. Add the curry paste and stir for 2 minutes. Pour in the coconut milk and heat until just boiling. Reduce the heat to a simmer and add the pumpkin, fish sauce and lime zest and juice. Cook for 10 minutes or until the pumpkin is fork tender. Add the green beans, tomatoes and pineapple and cook for 2 minutes. Scatter with the coriander and serve with the rice.

PREP AHEAD

The curry is best made on the night of serving. It can be frozen but be sure to undercook the pumpkin so it doesn't go mushy when reheating.

THE SKINNY

Thai red curry paste is a delish skinny ingredient to use in curries or as a rub on vegetables, fish or meats.

Wholemeal linguine with broccoli, garlic, chilli and lemon

preparation time 5 minutes / cooking time 10 minutes / serves 4

As a poor university student, my staple dinner was garlic spaghetti. It was simply olive oil, garlic and noodles. Parmesan was too dear, so I learnt to love this dish on its own with lots of black pepper. My grown-up version has less oil and more goodies thrown in. Nutty garlic, red chilli and lashings of lemon are tossed with the linguine and broccoli for an extraordinary but simple pasta.

350 g (12 oz) wholemeal (whole-wheat) linguine
3 tablespoons extra virgin olive oil
1 thumb-sized red chilli, thinly sliced
3 garlic cloves, sliced into coins
finely grated zest and juice of 2 lemons
300 g (10½ oz) broccolini or purple broccoli, cut into pieces
grated parmesan (optional)

Bring a large saucepan of salted water to the boil. Add the pasta and cook until al dente.

Meanwhile, heat the olive oil in a heavy-based frying pan over medium–low heat. Add the chilli and garlic and cook for 1 minute or until the garlic is golden. Remove from the heat and add the lemon zest and juice.

About 4 minutes before the pasta is done, add the broccoli to the same pan as the pasta. Drain when both are ready. Return to the pan and pour the garlic–chilli mixture over. Mix well, season to taste and scatter over a little parmesan if desired.

PREP AHEAD

This dish is best made on the night of serving.

THE SKINNY

Adding lemon juice to the garlic oil means you have more flavour without having to use more oil. The lemon also adds a zingy freshness without being too puckery.

Saffron risotto with tomato and spinach

preparation time 10 minutes / cooking time 25 minutes / serves 4

A good pinch of luxurious saffron makes a weekday meal feel ultra special. A little bag of fresh spinach thrown in at the end makes it a complete meal with vegetables. Be sure to taste your stock before you use it, checking if it is too watery or salty. That's often where risotto goes wrong. If it tastes good to start with, it will produce great risotto.

1.4 litres (49 fl oz) good-quality
   vegetable stock
1 teaspoon boiling water
1 large pinch of saffron threads, crushed
2 teaspoons olive oil
1 onion, chopped
275 g (9¾ oz) arborio rice
125 ml (4 fl oz/½ cup) white wine
3 roma (plum) tomatoes, seeds removed
   and chopped
200 g (7 oz) baby spinach leaves
4 tablespoons grated parmesan

Heat the stock in a large saucepan until boiling, then reduce to a simmer. Pour the boiling water over the saffron and allow to soak. Heat the olive oil in a separate large heavy-based saucepan over medium heat and sauté the onions with a bit of sea salt and freshly ground black pepper for 3–4 minutes or until translucent.

Add the rice and sauté for 3 minutes or until the grains are glistening. Pour in the saffron and soaking water and stir a minute, then add the wine. Stir until absorbed. Add one ladleful of stock and stir again until absorbed. Continue this process for about 10–15 minutes or until you have used nearly all of the stock and the rice is cooked but has a tiny bite to it. Add the tomato and spinach, check the seasoning and stir again. Scatter with the parmesan.

PREP AHEAD

This dish is best made on the night of serving.

THE SKINNY

Risotto is still delicious and far less gluey without loads of parmesan. You only need a little for that nutty gorgeous taste.

Mexican beans and rice with avocado salsa

preparation time 10 minutes / cooking time 15 minutes / serves 4–6

Whenever I eat Mexican fast food I like to order a 'taco rice bowl'. Instead of a tortilla shell, all the same ingredients are put into a bowl. I decided to make it at home as it's so more-ish and filling. I have played around with the trad 'beans and rice', stewing the beans in a garlicky, smoky chipotle, vinegar and honey sauce instead of pork fat. It's served up with warm rice and a chunky avocado salsa.

300 g (10½ oz/1½ cups) brown
   or white basmati rice
1 teaspoon olive oil
3 garlic cloves, chopped
1 small red onion, finely diced
2 x 400 g (14 oz) tins borlotti or pinto
   beans, drained and rinsed
3 teaspoons chipotle purée or chipotle
   Tabasco sauce
75 ml (2⅛ fl oz) apple cider vinegar
2 tablespoons honey
lime wedges and chipotle Tabasco
   sauce, to serve

Avocado salsa
2 avocados, cut into chunky pieces
1 small red onion, finely diced
3 tablespoons chopped coriander
   (cilantro)
juice of 1 lime

Place the rice in a large saucepan and cover with 7 cm (2¾ inches) water. Bring to the boil, then reduce the heat and simmer for 15–20 minutes or until al dente. Drain, then return to the pan. Cover with a lid to keep warm until using.

Heat the olive oil in a heavy-based saucepan over medium heat. Add the garlic and onion and cook for 5 minutes or until golden. Add the beans, chipotle purée, vinegar, honey and some sea salt and freshly ground black pepper. Sauté for 5 minutes or until the flavours come together.

To make the avocado salsa, mix the avocado, onion, coriander and lime juice together.

Divide the rice among plates, spoon the beans over and top with the salsa. Serve with the lime wedges and Tabasco sauce.

PREP AHEAD

The bean mixture can be made 1 day ahead and refrigerated or frozen — just thaw in the fridge on the day of using. Make the salsa just before serving to keep the colour of the avocado green.

THE SKINNY

Beans, when combined with rice, make a complete protein keeping you full. The garlic, vinegar and chilli keep the sauce skinny without saturated fat or excess oil.

Risotto primavera

preparation time 10 minutes / cooking time 25 minutes / serves 4

This classic green and orange speckled risotto is a slimmer version of the retro seventies cream-laden recipe, but being skinny doesn't mean it's lost any of its impressiveness.

- 1.4 litres (49 fl oz) good-quality vegetable stock
- 1 tablespoon olive oil
- 1 onion, finely chopped
- 2 large carrots, cut into 2 cm (¾ inch) dice
- 2 zucchini (courgettes), cut into 2 cm (¾ inch) dice
- 275 g (9¾ oz/1¼ cups) arborio rice
- 100 g (3½ oz) fresh or frozen shelled peas
- 6 spring onions (scallions), finely chopped
- 4 tablespoons grated parmesan

Heat the stock in a large saucepan until boiling, then reduce to a simmer. Heat the olive oil in a separate large heavy-based saucepan over medium heat and sauté the onion, carrot and zucchini along with some sea salt and freshly ground black pepper for 3–4 minutes or until the onion is translucent.

Add the rice and sauté for 3 minutes or until the grains are glistening. Add one ladleful of stock and stir until absorbed. Continue this process for about 15 minutes or until you have used nearly all of the stock and the rice is cooked but has a tiny bite to it. About 5 minutes before the rice is ready, add the peas and spring onion. Serve each portion with a tablespoon of parmesan.

PREP AHEAD

This is best made on the night of serving.

THE SKINNY

Risotto is mistakingly thought of as fattening but it is quite healthy and if the parmesan is kept to a minimum (as it is here — only 1 tablespoon per person), it's pretty slim. This is a great all-in-one dish with three of your five-a-day vegetables.

Polenta with roasted eggplant, tomato and olive sauce

preparation time 15 minutes / **cooking time** 30 minutes / **serves** 4

Creamy polenta (minus the cream and butter) is topped with a garlicky tomato and olive sauce and chunks of golden roasted eggplant for an Italian meatless meal. You could also use roasted butternut pumpkin and crisp leaves of sage if you're not an eggplant lover.

2 eggplant (aubergines), cut into 3 cm (1¼ inch) chunks
2 tablespoons olive oil
3 garlic cloves, chopped
1 large pinch of chilli flakes
2 x 400 g (14 oz) tins whole roma (plum) tomatoes
8 oil-cured black olives, pitted and halved
1 litre (35 fl oz/4 cups) vegetable stock
200 g (7 oz) instant polenta
4 tablespoons grated parmesan
4 handfuls rocket (arugula) leaves, to serve

Preheat the oven to 190°C (375°F/Gas 5). Toss the eggplant with 1 tablespoon of the olive oil. Season well with sea salt and freshly ground black pepper and spread out on a large baking tray. Roast for 25 minutes or until golden.

Heat the remaining olive oil in a saucepan over medium heat. Add the garlic and chilli flakes and sauté for 2 minutes or until golden. Add the tomatoes, a good teaspoon of salt and cook for 10 minutes or until thickened. Add the olives in the last 5 minutes of cooking. Reduce the heat to low and keep warm.

Heat the stock in a saucepan. When it comes to the boil, slowly add the polenta. Stir until it has thickened, about 1–2 minutes. Add half of the parmesan and stir again. Serve up four bowls with the polenta. Pour some warm tomato and olive sauce over and scatter with the roasted eggplant. Place a handful of rocket on each and scatter with the remaining parmesan.

PREP AHEAD

This dish is best made on the night of serving.

THE SKINNY

The polenta has been stripped down here and made without the usual butter or cream but it still tastes very good lushed up with stock and parmesan.

Roasted harissa vegetables with kale, chilli and ginger pilaf

preparation time 15 minutes / cooking time 30 minutes / serves 4

Harissa works as an instant rub for these roasted vegetables served up with a ginger and kale pilaf and Greek yoghurt. Any vegetables can be used here, such as eggplant (aubergine) or zucchini (courgette).

1 small butternut pumpkin (winter squash) (about 1 kg/2 lb 4 oz), peeled and cut into 3 cm (1¼ inch) chunks
2 red onions, quartered
2 red capsicums (peppers), cut into 3 cm (1¼ inch) pieces
1–2 tablespoons harissa paste, or to taste
low-fat Greek yoghurt, to serve

Kale, ginger and chilli pilaf
1 tablespoon olive oil
1 onion, thinly sliced
2 garlic cloves, chopped
3 cm (1¼ inch) piece of ginger, peeled and finely chopped
1 thumb-sized red chilli, seeds removed and sliced
200 g (7 oz) kale or other greens, chopped
200 g (7 oz/1 cup) basmati rice
450 ml (16 fl oz) vegetable stock

Preheat the oven to 200°C (400°F/Gas 6). Place the pumpkin, onion and capsicum on a large baking tray or two smaller ones. Toss them with the harissa and season with sea salt and freshly ground black pepper. Roast for 30 minutes or until golden and tender.

Meanwhile, make the kale, ginger and chilli pilaf. Heat the olive oil in a saucepan over medium heat, add the onion, garlic, ginger and chilli and season. Sauté for 5 minutes or until the onion is translucent. Add the kale, rice and stock. Bring to the boil, reduce the heat to low, cover with a lid and cook for 8 minutes or until tender. Serve with the roasted vegetables and some yoghurt alongside.

PREP AHEAD

This is best made on the night of serving.

THE SKINNY

Four portions of vegetables and rice make this sing with health, but more importantly it's an aromatic, delicious rice spiked with ginger and chilli.

Sweet and sour red lentil dhal with roasted eggplant

preparation time 10 minutes / cooking time 30 minutes / serves 4

⁓⁓⁓⁓⁓⁓⁓⁓⁓⁓⁓⁓⁓⁓⁓

Indian dhal is cheap as chips, good for you and full of solace. Golden chunks of roasted eggplant add a meaty texture but you can substitute any vegetable you like, such as roasted pumpkin, blanched green beans or even diced carrots.

1 eggplant (aubergine), cut into 3 cm (1¼ inch) chunks
3 tablespoons vegetable oil
200 g (7 oz) red lentils
1 teaspoon ground turmeric
1 litre (35 fl oz/4 cups) vegetable stock or water
1 brown onion, thinly sliced
2 garlic cloves, finely chopped
1 tablespoon finely grated ginger
2 teaspoons garam masala or curry powder
100 g (3½ oz) tamarind purée
steamed basmati rice, lime pickle or chutney and coriander (cilantro) leaves, to serve

Preheat the oven to 190°C (375°F/Gas 5). Toss the eggplant chunks with 1 tablespoon of the vegetable oil and season well with sea salt and freshly ground black pepper. Roast for 20 minutes or until golden.

Meanwhile, rinse the lentils and place in a saucepan. Add the turmeric and stock and season with salt. Bring to the boil over high heat and cook for 15 minutes or until very soft. Skim any foam that may form on the top.

Heat the remaining vegetable oil in a heavy-based frying pan over medium heat. Add the onion, garlic and ginger, season and cook for 5 minutes or until golden. Add the garam masala and sauté for 2 minutes. Add the tamarind purée and the cooked lentils and simmer for 5 minutes.

Serve with the eggplant, rice and lime pickle or chutney with the coriander scattered over.

· ·

PREP AHEAD

The dhal can be made up to 2 days ahead and refrigerated. It may need thinning out with a bit of stock or water. It can also be frozen.

THE SKINNY

Eaten with rice, lentils make a complete protein. They require hardly any oil to cook and the ginger, garlic, onion and spice give them a kick.

Zucchini, tomato and onion gratin with crisp breadcrumbs

preparation time 15 minutes / cooking time 40 minutes / serves 4

Growing up in Wisconsin, my dad, Leo, had a bursting vegetable garden. At the end of summer, we had crate upon crate of zucchini. I would secretly curse them because my sisters and I would have to can, pickle and cook them for days. This was one of my mother's magical recipes on how to use them up. The slices are stewed in a sweet tomato–onion sauce and the parmesan breadcrumbs (my addition) add some crunch.

3 tablespoons olive oil

2 large brown onions, thinly sliced into half moons

3 garlic cloves, chopped

1 large pinch of chilli flakes

2 x 400 g (14 oz) tins whole roma (plum) tomatoes

4 zucchini (courgettes), cut into 1 cm (½ inch) thick slices

2 handfuls fresh sourdough breadcrumbs

2 tablespoons grated parmesan

Preheat the oven to 190°C (375°F/Gas 5). Heat 2 tablespoons of the olive oil in a large saucepan over medium–high heat. Add the onion, garlic and chilli flakes, season with sea salt and freshly ground black pepper and sauté for 10 minutes or until light golden. Add the tomatoes and break up with a spoon. Cook for 10 minutes or until thick. Add the zucchini and pour into a 30 cm x 23 cm (12 inch x 9 inch) baking dish. Toss the breadcrumbs with the remaining olive oil and parmesan and season. Spread over the top of the zucchini mixture and bake for 20 minutes or until crisp and golden.

PREP AHEAD

The entire gratin can be made 4 hours ahead and refrigerated, then reheated. Otherwise prepare it 2 hours ahead and bake before eating.

THE SKINNY

Only a small amount of parmesan is used in the breadcrumbs to add more taste. Since the zucchini are baked in the tomato sauce, very little oil is used.

Squid ink spaghetti with fennel, cherry tomatoes and basil

preparation time 10 minutes / cooking time 20 minutes / serves 4

Squid ink spaghetti doesn't really taste that much different than plain pasta but its noir colour is striking. With some white fennel, basil and cherry tomatoes, it's even more stunning. But more important than beauty, it's a lovely dish to devour. Substitute regular pasta if you like.

2 tablespoons extra virgin olive oil
4 garlic cloves, finely chopped
1 large pinch of chilli flakes
4 small fennel bulbs, cores removed, thinly sliced and chopped
250 g (9 oz) cherry tomatoes, halved
400 g (14 oz) dried squid ink spaghetti
1 small handful basil leaves, torn
2 tablespoons grated parmesan

Heat the olive oil in a large frying pan over medium heat, add the garlic, chilli and fennel. Season well with sea salt and freshly ground black pepper and sauté for 15 minutes or until softened. Add the tomato, season again and cook for 5 minutes or until the tomatoes break down a bit.

Meanwhile, cook the pasta in a large saucepan of salted boiling water until al dente, then drain. Add to the sauce with the basil. Serve in bowls with parmesan scattered over.

PREP AHEAD

This is best made on the night of serving.

THE SKINNY

These are all lean tasty ingredients with little fat. Just a small sprinkling of parmesan gives you the nutty taste of the cheese without copious calories. For more protein, throw some white crabmeat or prawns into the sauce just when it's nearly ready.

Coriander potato cakes with mango chutney

preparation time 15 minutes / cooking time 20 minutes / serves 4

You won't be yearning for meat with these spice-kissed potato cakes studded with spring onion, lemon rind and bits of melty cheese. They taste fried with their crisp breadcrumbs but are very chaste indeed.

500 g (1 lb 2 oz) floury potatoes, peeled
1 egg, separated
1 handful coriander (cilantro) leaves, chopped
6 small spring onions (scallions), thinly sliced
zest of 1 lemon
75 g (2⅝ oz) low-fat cheddar, grated
1 thumb-sized red chilli, seeds removed and chopped
80 g (2¾ oz) dried fine breadcrumbs, toasted
1 tablespoon vegetable oil
mango chutney and green salad, to serve

Cook the potatoes in salted boiling water until they start to fall apart. Drain and place back in the warm pan to dry out for a few minutes. Mash the potato, egg yolk, coriander and spring onion together, season with sea salt and freshly ground black pepper and mix in the lemon zest, cheddar and chilli. Shape into 8 cakes.

Place the eggwhite in a bowl and whisk until foamy. Place the breadcrumbs on a plate. Dip the cakes in the eggwhite, allow the excess to drain off, then coat in the breadcrumbs, pressing to adhere well. Place on a tray lined with baking paper, cover and refrigerate until using.

Heat the vegetable oil in a large heavy-based non-stick frying pan over medium heat. Cook the cakes in batches for 2–3 minutes each side or until golden and heated through. Serve with the chutney and salad.

PREP AHEAD

The cakes can be made 1 day ahead and refrigerated or frozen — thaw in the fridge. Pan-fry just before you want to eat them.

THE SKINNY

Vegetable cakes don't have to be hugely caloric if you use a good heavy-based non-stick frying pan. It will conduct the heat better and you won't need as much oil. Just keep the temperature low so that they brown slowly.

Grilled wasabi salmon with chunky cucumber and poppy seed salad

preparation time 10 minutes / **cooking time** 5 minutes / **serves** 4

Spicy wasabi makes a glaze for grilled fish in the bat of an eye. The cucumber salad, with its crunchy poppy seeds, chilli and rice vinegar dressing, creates a refreshing side.

4 x 125 g (4½ oz) pieces of salmon
    with skin, pin-boned
1 teaspoon vegetable oil
2 tablespoons wasabi paste
1 telegraph (long) cucumber
1 thumb-sized red chilli, cut into rounds
2 tablespoons rice wine vinegar
1 tablespoon caster (superfine) sugar
1 tablespoon poppy seeds
1 tablespoon sea salt
steamed rice, to serve

Rub both sides of the salmon with a tiny bit of the vegetable oil and then the wasabi paste. Halve the cucumber lengthways and remove the seeds. Cut the flesh diagonally into 4 cm (1½ inch) chunks and place in a bowl. Add the chilli, vinegar, sugar, poppy seeds, salt and a bit of freshly ground black pepper. Mix to disslove the sugar and salt.

Preheat the grill (broiler) to high. Cook the salmon fillets, skin side down, without turning for 5–6 minutes, depending on their thickness. Serve with the salad and the steamed rice.

PREP AHEAD

You can coat the fish 1 day ahead and refrigerate or freeze. Thaw in the refrigerator before cooking. Mix the salad just before eating.

THE SKINNY

Wasabi, like other Asian pastes, makes a zero fat glaze and complements salmon's rich character.

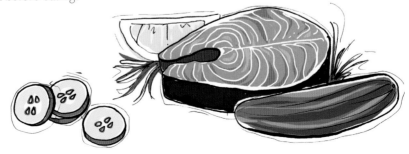

Spaghetti with red clam sauce and gremolata

preparation time 10 minutes / soaking time 1 hour / cooking time 15 minutes / serves 4

Some red clam sauces have a long list of ingredients but this one is dead simple with the clams steamed right on top of the garlicky tomato sauce. It all relies on getting little baby clams that are tender and delicate. The bigger ones are too rubbery. A sharp lemon and parsley gremolata is sprinkled over for a knockout pasta.

600 g (1 lb 5 oz) baby clams (vongole)
1 tablespoon sea salt
1 tablespoon olive oil
2 anchovy fillets, rinsed
1 large pinch of chilli flakes
4 garlic cloves, chopped
3 x 400 g (14 oz) tins whole roma
    (plum) tomatoes
400 g (14 oz) spaghetti
finely grated zest of 1 lemon
2 tablespoons chopped flat-leaf
    (Italian) parsley

Cover the clams with water, add the salt and refrigerate for 1 hour, agitating the clams regularly. This helps them to 'burp up' any sand they have inside.

Heat the olive oil in a large saucepan with a fitted lid over medium heat. Add the anchovy fillets, chilli and garlic and sauté for 2 minutes or until golden. Add the tomatoes and break up with a spoon. Cook for 10 minutes or until slightly thickened and reduced. Season to taste.

Cook the pasta in salted boiling water until al dente. In the last 5 minutes of the pasta cooking, add the clams to the tomato sauce, keeping them mostly on top of the sauce, cover with the lid and steam until they open.

Drain the pasta and add to the tomato sauce. Cook for a few minutes, then toss through the lemon zest and parsley.

PREP AHEAD

This is best made on the night of serving.

THE SKINNY

Seafood like clams are packed with flavourful juices that don't add any calories. The lemon and parsley cut through the richness keeping it fresh and light.

Prawn tacos with black beans and pickled jalapeño salsa

preparation time 15 minutes / cooking time 10 minutes / serves 4

Make fresh tomato salsa a little more exciting, by stirring through some chopped pickled jalapeño (green chilli peppers). It will make any taco or Mexican dish infinitely better. Substitute firm white fish fillets or chicken in place of the prawns if you like. Roll everything up in a soft flour tortilla or make the crisp oven-baked ones (see page 109).

500 g (1 lb 2 oz) large peeled prawns (shrimp), butterflied
1 teaspoon ground cumin
1 teaspoon chilli powder
2 x 400 g (14 oz) tins black beans, drained and rinsed
1 teaspoon vegetable oil
1 lime, halved
fresh corn or flour tortillas , low-fat Greek yoghurt, chopped coriander (cilantro) and Tabasco sauce, to serve

Jalapeño salsa
1 small red onion, finely diced
2 limes, one juiced and the other halved
2 tablespoons chopped pickled jalapeños or 1 chopped green chilli
1 handful coriander (cilantro) leaves, chopped
200 g (7 oz) cherry tomatoes, quartered

To make the jalapeño salsa, place the onion in a bowl and pour over the lime juice. Allow to sit for 5 minutes, then add the pickled jalapeño, coriander and tomato. Season with sea salt and freshly ground black pepper and set aside.

Preheat the oven to 200°C (400°F/Gas 6).

Mix the prawns with the spices and season.

Heat the beans in a saucepan over low heat, slightly mashing them.

Warm the tortillas in foil in the oven for 5 minutes.

Heat the vegetable oil in a large frying pan over high heat. Cook the prawns about 1 minute each side, then squeeze over the lime halves.

To serve, spoon some of the black beans over each tortilla, top with the prawns, salsa, yoghurt, some coriander and a good dash of Tabasco.

PREP AHEAD

The salsa can be made a couple of hours ahead. The rest should be done just before serving.

THE SKINNY

All the ingredients here are virtuous. Refried beans, which normally entail lard, are replaced with warm black beans and Greek yoghurt stands in for the sour cream.

Bengali salmon parcels with mustard-yoghurt paste

preparation time 15 minutes / cooking time 10 minutes / serves 4

Any firm fish will work with this simple Indian yoghurt marinade of ginger, green chillies and wholegrain mustard. Traditionally it's a recipe that involves mustard oil but it's a tricky ingredient to find so I've devised my own interpretation. Eat with fragrant basmati rice and fat wedges of lemon to squeeze over everything.

4 x 125 g (4½ oz) pieces of skinless
   salmon fillet, pin-boned
1 teaspoon ground turmeric
1 teaspoon ground cumin
3 cm (1¼ inch) piece of ginger, peeled
   and sliced
1 garlic clove
1 small handful coriander (cilantro),
   chopped
2 thumb-sized green chillies, seeds
   removed and sliced
2 tablespoons wholegrain mustard
200 g (7 oz) low-fat Greek yoghurt,
   plus extra to serve
steamed basmati rice and lemon
   wedges, to serve

Preheat a barbecue to high or the oven to 200°C (400°F/Gas 6). Rub the salmon with the turmeric and season with sea salt and freshly ground black pepper. Place the ginger, garlic, coriander and nearly all of the chilli in a food processor and process until finely chopped. Add the mustard, half of the yoghurt and some sea salt and pulse to combine.

Prepare four doubled sheets of foil. Spread the paste on both sides of the fish pieces. Place a piece on one half of a sheet, then bring the other half over and fold in the sides to make a parcel and seal. Repeat with the remaining fish.

Cook the parcels for 8–10 minutes. Open one to check if the fish is done; if not, seal up again and give it another minute or two. For thicker fish, you may need a few more minutes. Serve with the rice, yoghurt and lemon wedges.

PREP AHEAD

The fish can be marinated 1 day ahead and refrigerated or frozen — simply thaw in the fridge the day before.

THE SKINNY

Low-fat Greek yoghurt and mustard are the star skinny ingredients in this Indian marinade and they're all guilt-free.

Stir-fried fish with dill and rice noodles

preparation time 15 minutes / cooking time 5 minutes / serves 4

This delicious Vietnamese specialty is called cha ca. An entire street in Hanoi is dedicated to restaurants that specialise in it. My family and I visited there quite a few times on our trip. The turmeric and garlic–marinated fish is stir-fried with copious amounts of dill including the stalks. It's eaten over rice noodles with pickled red chillies, herbs and crushed peanuts and is utterly divine. Totally simple and amazing. Be sure to use fish that is thick and non-flaky and that can withstand stir-frying.

1 small onion, coarsely grated

2 garlic cloves, chopped

2.5 cm (1 inch) piece of ginger, finely chopped

2 teaspoons ground turmeric

2 tablespoons fish sauce

2 tablespoons peanut oil

900 g (2 lb) piece of skinless barramundi, red snapper, monkfish or tilapia fillet, cut into 4 cm (1½ inch) chunks

200 g (7 oz) dried rice vermicelli noodles

6 spring onions (scallions), thinly sliced

40 g (1½ oz/⅔ cup) roughly chopped dill stalks and leaves

chopped roasted peanuts, coriander (cilantro) sprigs, sliced red chilli marinated in rice vinegar and lime cheeks, to serve

Combine the onion, garlic, ginger, turmeric, fish sauce and 1 teaspoon of the peanut oil in a bowl. Mix well, then add the fish and allow to marinate for 10 minutes.

Meanwhile, place the noodles in a large bowl and pour over boiling water to cover well. Leave to sit for about 5 minutes or until tender, then drain.

Heat the remaining peanut oil in a large wok over high heat. Add the spring onion and dill and cook for 1 minute, then add the fish mixture. Stir-fry for 3–4 minutes or until the fish is cooked through.

Divide the noodles among bowls and serve the fish on top with its juices spooned over. Serve with a small sprinkling of peanuts, the coriander, chilli vinegar and lime cheeks.

PREP AHEAD

The fish can be marinated up to 3 hours before or frozen in the marinade.

THE SKINNY

The fresh herbs, turmeric and fish sauce provide punch without the fat and the rice noodles keep this dish filling.

Sicilian fish and couscous stew

preparation time 10 minutes / cooking time 20 minutes / serves 4

In Trapani, Sicily, where this fish stew was created, they throw in whole fish. Although the heads, tails and bones add flavour to the base, they aren't much fun to fish out. This is my modern interpretation but it is still reminiscent of the delicious seaside stew.

100 g (3½ oz) fregola or regular couscous
125 ml (4 fl oz/½ cup) boiling water
2 tablespoons olive oil
2 onions, thinly sliced
4 celery stalks, thinly sliced
4 garlic cloves, sliced
1 anchovy fillet
1 pinch of chilli flakes
4 large roma (plum) tomatoes, seeds removed and diced
250 ml (9 fl oz/1 cup) white wine
800 ml (28 fl oz) vegetable stock
4 x 125 g (4½ oz) red mullet or other firm white fish fillets, skin on and bones removed
finely grated zest of 1 lemon
2 tablespoons chopped flat-leaf (Italian) parsley

If using fregola, cook it in salted boiling water for about 5 minutes or until al dente. Drain and set aside. If using couscous, mix it with the water, season with sea salt and freshly ground black pepper, cover and allow to sit.

Heat the olive oil in a large saucepan over medium heat, add the onion, celery, garlic, anchovy fillet and chilli flakes, season and sauté for 10 minutes or until light golden. Add the tomato and sauté for another couple of minutes. Pour in the wine and stock and bring to the boil. Reduce the heat to a simmer and add the fish. Cover with a lid and cook for 5 minutes or until the fish is cooked.

If using fregola, add it to the pan. If using couscous, break it up with your fingers and add it to the pan. Divide among large serving bowls and scatter with the lemon zest and parsley.

PREP AHEAD

The stew base and boiled fregola can be prepared 1 day ahead and refrigerated. Add the fish just before serving.

THE SKINNY

A tomato base for fish is tasty, doesn't require too much starchy pasta and uses very little oil.

Seared scallops with crushed potatoes and lemon-chilli sauce

preparation time 10 minutes / cooking time 15 minutes / serves 4

I made this dish for my friend Sarah Birks who christened it 'healthy posh nosh'. If bought in season, scallops won't be expensive. Not just for special occasions, they make an incredibly fast and light dinner. Crushed potatoes mixed with greens are the base for these decadent molluscs and a warm lemon, caper and chilli dressing brings it all together.

500 g (1 lb 2 oz) baby (new) potatoes
100 g (3½ oz) cavolo nero (Tuscan black kale) or savoy cabbage, centre veins discarded, leaves thinly sliced
3 tablespoons extra virgin olive oil
1 tablespoon baby capers, rinsed
3 garlic cloves, thinly sliced
2 thumb-sized red chillies, seeds removed and sliced
juice of 1 lemon
12 large scallops, orange roe removed

Cook the potatoes in salted boiling water for 10 minutes. Add the cavolo nero in the last 2–3 minutes. Drain and place back in the pan. Drizzle with 1 teaspoon of the oil, season with sea salt and roughly mash together. Keep warm while you make the sauce and cook the scallops.

Heat 2 tablespoons of the olive oil in a small frying pan over medium–high heat. Add the capers, garlic and chilli and sauté for 1–2 minutes or until golden. Remove from the heat and add the lemon juice. Place back on the heat and reduce for 1 minute.

Heat the remaining olive oil in a heavy-based frying pan over high heat. When very hot, add the scallops, season with sea salt and freshly ground black pepper and sear for 1 minute each side or until golden brown but not cooked all the way through (scallops are best cooked this way but cook them through if you like). Remove and serve with the potatoes and the sauce poured over.

PREP AHEAD

The sauce and potatoes can be made a couple of hours ahead. Sear the scallops at the last minute.

THE SKINNY

The lemon in the sauce keeps it skinny without extra oil and cuts through the richness of the scallops. When lemon juice is allowed to sizzle in the pan, it loses its acidity.

Grilled tuna steaks with ponzu sauce and granny smith apple salad

preparation time 10 minutes / cooking time 5 minutes / serves 4

Ponzu sauce is a Japanese dipping sauce,which consists of soy sauce, citrus juice and sugar. It's mainly used as a condiment for fried food, but I love it for dipping and as a marinade or tart dressing. Grilled tuna and the tart apple and celery salad soak up the tangy ginger-infused sauce for a winning trio.

75 ml (2⅛ fl oz) Japanese soy sauce
juice of 2 limes
1 tablespoon caster (superfine) sugar
4 x 125 g (4½ oz) tuna steaks
1 tablespoon finely chopped ginger
1 teaspoon vegetable oil
steamed rice, to serve

Granny smith salad
2 granny smith apples, cores removed
    and cut into julienne
4 handfuls watercress sprigs
2 celery stalks, cut into thin matchsticks
4 spring onions (scallions), thinly sliced

Mix together the soy, nearly all of the lime juice (reserving a little for the salad) and all of the sugar. Spoon a bit over the tuna and rub it into the flesh, along with the ginger and vegetable oil. Season with sea salt and freshly ground black pepper. Reserve the remaining marinade for serving.

Preheat a barbecue, grill (broiler) or chargrill (griddle) pan to high.

To make the salad, mix the apple with the reserved lime juice and toss with the watercress, celery and spring onion.

Cook the tuna for 1–1½ minutes each side, keeping the centre fairly rare. Serve with the salad and the marinade poured over. Serve with the rice.

PREP AHEAD

The tuna marinade can be made the day before. Everything else should be done shortly before eating.

THE SKINNY

The lime counters the saltiness of the soy and makes a slim dressing for both the tuna and the salad.

Salmon and horseradish pies with crisp potato crust

preparation time 20 minutes / cooking time 35 minutes / serves 4

Skinny comfort food? Yes, it can be done. One wouldn't expect to find a fish pie in a healthy food cookbook but it just goes to show anything is possible. A golden potato crust replaces the traditional pastry, and spring onion, horseradish, dill and lemon zest bolster the béchamel for a full-on flavoured pie. Be sure to use flaky smoked fillets, not the thinly sliced type.

2–3 red-skinned potatoes, scrubbed
  and cut into 5 mm (¼ inch) slices
25 g (1 oz) unsalted butter
1 large bunch spring onions (scallions),
  chopped
3 tablespoons plain (all-purpose) flour
750 ml (26 fl oz/3 cups) skim milk
2 tablespoons prepared horseradish,
  or to taste
2 tablespoons chopped dill
finely grated zest of 1 lemon
400 g (14 oz) hot-smoked salmon
  or trout, skin and bones removed,
  flesh broken into big chunks
olive oil spray

Preheat the oven to 200°C (400°F/Gas 6).

Bring a saucepan of salted water to the boil. Drop in the potato slices and cook for 3 minutes or until just al dente. Drain well and lay out on a tray lined with a tea towel to dry.

Melt the butter in a saucepan over medium–low heat. Add the spring onion and sauté for 2 minutes. Whisk in the flour and cook for 1 minute. Season with sea salt and freshly ground black pepper and whisk in the milk and horseradish. Bring to the boil and allow to thicken for a couple of minutes, then add a good teaspoon of salt, the dill, lemon zest and fish.

Pour into four 300 ml (10½ fl oz) capacity pie dishes. Layer the potatoes over, slightly overlapping like fish scales and spray with the oil. Place on a baking tray, season and bake for 20–25 minutes or until golden and bubbly.

PREP AHEAD

The pie mixture can be made 1 day ahead and refrigerated or frozen. If freezing, leave the potatoes off since they don't freeze well. Thaw the pies in the refrigerator on the day of cooking.

THE SKINNY

Pot pies don't have to be calorie crushers. Using skim milk for the béchamel keeps it light but still provides a thick sauce. Lemon zest and horseradish pump it full of flavour and counter the rich fish.

Fish tray bake with potato, fennel and tomato-olive vinaigrette

preparation time 10 minutes / cooking time 40 minutes / serves 4

For so little effort, there is a lot of payback here. Whack it in the oven to roast and spoon the tomato, olive and shallot dressing over the crisp potato and fish. It's important to use oil-cured Italian olives, not Kalamata as they are too salty and overpower the taste of the other ingredients.

500 g (1 lb 2 oz) small kipfler potatoes, scrubbed and cut into 1.5 cm (⅝ inch) slices
4 small fennel bulbs, cores removed and thickly sliced
1 tablespoon extra virgin olive oil
4 x 125 g (4½ oz) pieces of salmon, halibut, tilapia or other fish fillets
1 teaspoon fennel seeds, slightly crushed

Tomato-olive vinaigrette
1 tablespoon white balsamic vinegar or white wine vinegar
2 French shallots (eschalots), thinly sliced
2 tablespoons extra virgin olive oil
2 roma (plum) tomatoes, seeds removed and diced
15 oil-cured black olives, pitted and roughly chopped

Preheat the oven to 200°C (400°F/Gas 6).

Arrange the potato and fennel slices in a single layer on a large baking tray. Drizzle with the olive oil and season with sea salt and freshly ground black pepper. Bake for 30 minutes or until golden and nearly cooked through, then place the fish on top and sprinkle with the fennel seeds and more seasoning. Bake for another 10 minutes or until the fish is cooked.

Meanwhile, make the tomato-olive vinaigrette. Pour the vinegar over the shallot in a bowl and allow to sit for a few minutes, then add the olive oil, tomato and olives and season. Mix well and set aside.

Serve the potato, fennel and fish bake with the vinaigrette spooned over.

PREP AHEAD

This meal is best made just before eating.

THE SKINNY

Roasting vegetables makes them crisp but very low in fat. The vinaigrette is a tasty skinny sauce to replace mayonnaise or crème fraîche-based sauces.

Southern red rice prawns with celery and tomatoes

preparation time 15 minutes / cooking time 30 minutes / serves 4

Creole food relies on staple spices like bay, celery salt and cayenne, which make their cuisine so addictive. One of my favourite dishes is jambalaya, which has a hefty list of ingredients. This is a much simpler, leaner rendition but just as mouth-watering.

3 slices lean bacon, chopped
1 tablespoon olive oil
1 large brown onion, finely chopped
1 red capsicum (pepper), chopped
    into 2 cm (¾ inch) pieces
3 celery stalks, cut into 2 cm (¾ inch)
    thick slices
1 teaspoon celery salt
4 fresh bay leaves
1 x 400 g (14 oz) tin whole roma
    (plum) tomatoes
275 g (9¾ oz/1¼ cups) basmati rice
600 ml (21 fl oz) chicken stock
400 g (14 oz) large raw prawns
    (shrimp), peeled and deveined
chopped flat-leaf (Italian) parsley
    and lemon wedges, to serve

Cook the bacon in a heavy-based saucepan over high heat for 5 minutes or until crisp. Remove, drain on paper towel and discard the fat.

Add the olive oil to the pan, along with the onion, capsicum, celery and celery salt and cook over medium heat for 8–10 minutes or until soft. Add the bay leaves, tomatoes and rice and cook for another minute. Pour in the stock, cover with a lid, reduce the heat to low and cook for 10 minutes. Add the prawns and cook for 5 minutes. Scatter over the parsley and serve with the lemon wedges.

PREP AHEAD

This dish is best made just before eating.

THE SKINNY

Yes there is a tiny amount of bacon here but only 3 slices. That's enough to impart a smoky flavour and is the only caloric ingredient included. Turkey bacon, which is very low in fat can also be used.

Steamed lemon ginger fish with sticky teriyaki sauce

preparation time 15 minutes / cooking time 15 minutes / serves 4

This Japanese-inspired hotpot is a snap to put together. The fish is placed right on top of the cooking rice and showered with ginger, chillies and lemon. A thickened teriyaki sauce is poured over just before eating.

250 g (9 oz/1¼ cups) basmati rice

450 ml (16 fl oz) water

4 x 125 g (4½ oz) pieces of red snapper, tilapia or other fish fillets

3 cm (1¼ inch) piece of ginger, shredded

1 thumb-sized red chilli, seeds removed and sliced

1 lemon, halved and one-half thinly sliced

sliced spring onions (scallions), to garnish

Sticky teriyaki sauce

100 ml (3½ fl oz) Japanese soy sauce

100 ml (3½ fl oz) mirin

juice of ½ lemon

3 tablespoons white sugar

To make the sticky teriyaki sauce, place all the ingredients in a saucepan and bring to the boil. Simmer for 5 minutes or until slightly syrupy. Remove and set aside.

Rinse the rice in a saucepan about 2–3 times or until the water runs clear. Drain and cover with the water. Bring to the boil, then reduce the heat to a simmer and cook for about 5 minutes. When the rice has absorbed three-quarters of the water, place the fish fillets on top. Squeeze the lemon half over each piece of fish, then top with the ginger, chilli and a slice of lemon. Season with sea salt and freshly ground black pepper, cover with a lid and cook for about 5 minutes or until the fish is cooked.

Serve the fish and rice with the sauce poured over and the spring onion to garnish.

PREP AHEAD

The sauce can be made 1 day ahead and refrigerated. Thin with a bit of water when reheating.

THE SKINNY

Steaming is the perfect treatment for delicate fish and this entire dish doesn't require any oil.

Weekend Cooking

Lamb kleftiko

preparation time 10 minutes / cooking time 2½–3 hours / serves 4

All of these ingredients get wrapped up in a large parcel to steam and slow-roast for hours. It's little effort for a high return. Pop it in the oven, go for a walk and leave it to cook. When you open it, the meat flakes apart and the lemons are almost caramelised. Serve it with steamed rice or roasted chunky potatoes.

2 kg (4 lb 8 oz) piece of boneless lamb leg or shoulder, trimmed of all fat
1½ tablespoons olive oil
8 garlic cloves, halved
1 teaspoon ground cinnamon
1 tablespoon dried wild oregano
1 lemon, zest removed in wide strips and juiced
2 roma (plum) tomatoes, quartered
125 ml (4 fl oz/⅓ cup) white wine
Greek yoghurt and steamed rice or potatoes, to serve

Preheat the oven to 160°C (315°F/Gas 2–3). Cut the lamb into 13 cm (5 inch) pieces and season with sea salt and freshly ground black pepper. Heat the olive oil in a large frying pan over high heat until very hot. Sear the lamb on both sides until nicely browned. Using a pointy knife, make incisions in the lamb and push the garlic into the slits.

Tear off two sheets of foil about 1.2 metres (47 inches) long and place inside a roasting tray. Bring up the sides as if making a shallow bowl. Place the lamb in the centre and add the cinnamon, oregano, lemon zest and juice, tomato and wine. Season again, then fold over the edges of the foil to seal completely; make sure there is room for air to circulate but also that the foil is tight enough so the lamb steams as it cooks. Check the meat after 2½ hours and if it isn't meltingly tender, put it back in the oven for another 30 minutes. If it's dry, add a tiny bit more wine but it shouldn't need it. Serve with the yoghurt and rice or potatoes.

PREP AHEAD
The meat can be seared, cooled and sealed up on the morning of serving, ready to roast later.

THE SKINNY
Slow roasting requires hardly any oil.
If there is fat marbling in the meat it will melt out while cooking, leaving fork-tender flesh.

Poulet au poule with salsa verde

preparation time 15 minutes / **cooking time** 1½ hours / **serves** 4–6

This classic French dish is about as virtuous as food gets but it is utterly divine. The chicken cooks up snowy white and the vegetables so pure, it's a wonder why we don't poach food more often. Piquant herb salsa verde is served up alongside to drizzle over. Wafts of chicken stock will perfume your kitchen while it slowly bubbles away.

1.7 kg (3 lb 12 oz) whole chicken
1 onion, studded with 4 whole cloves
1 bouquet garni (thyme and parsley
   sprigs and a bay leaf tied together
   in a bundle)
4 large carrots, halved
2 leeks, cut into 10 cm (4 inch) pieces
3 small turnips, halved
cooked Puy (tiny blue-green) lentils,
   to serve (optional)

Salsa verde

3 tablespoons extra virgin olive oil
2 tablespoons red wine vinegar
1 teaspoon French wholegrain mustard
1 large handful flat-leaf (Italian) parsley
   leaves, chopped
3 cornichons (gherkins), diced

Rinse the chicken well, inside and out, and place in a large saucepan. Cover with water and add the onion, bouquet garni and a bit of sea salt. Bring to the boil, then reduce the heat to low and simmer for 1 hour. Add the vegetables and cook for another 30 minutes or until tender.

Meanwhile, make the salsa verde. Mix all the ingredients in a small bowl.

Remove the chicken and vegetables from the pan and place on a platter. Chop into pieces. Discard the chicken skin and bones. Serve with the salsa verde. Cooked Puy lentils are also nic

PREP AHEAD

The vegetables can be peeled and prepared on the morning of serving and kept in a bowl of cold water to keep them from discolouring.

THE SKINNY

Poaching meat or poultry keeps the flesh juicy and tender but no oil or fat is needed. The piquant salsa verde is also healthy and complements the chicken's mild taste.

Pork tenderloin with charred tomato and chipotle chilli sauce

preparation time 30 minutes / cooking time 30 minutes / serves 6

Authentic Mexican sauces use an ingenious technique called blackening. The onions and tomatoes are placed under the grill (broiler) or in a frying pan and cooked until blackened. When puréed with chillies, cider vinegar, sugar and spices, it creates an amazing smoky tomato sauce. Since most chipotle chillies are sold already puréed in little jars, they can go straight into the sauce. (You need to remove the skins of other types of chillies before using.)

2 x 500 g (1 lb 2 oz) pork tenderloins
    (fillets), sinew trimmed
1 tablespoon white sugar
1 teaspoon chilli powder, or to taste
    (ancho is nice but use any mild one)
fresh coriander (cilantro) leaves and
    lime-pickled onion (see page 76),
    to serve

Red sauce

3 roma (plum) tomatoes, halved
1 small brown onion, thickly sliced
4 large garlic cloves, unpeeled
1½ tablespoons apple cider vinegar
250 ml (9 fl oz/1 cup) water
¼ teaspoon dried wild oregano
¼ teaspoon ground cumin
1½ tablespoons chipotle purée
1½ tablespoons soft brown sugar

To make the red sauce, preheat the grill (broiler) to high. Arrange the tomato halves and onion slices in a large roasting tray lined with foil. Season with sea salt and freshly ground black pepper and grill for 10 minutes or until blackened. Remove and transfer to a blender or food processor.

Cook the garlic in their skins in a dry frying pan over medium heat for 8 minutes or until blackened on all sides. Allow to cool a little, then peel and add to the tomato mixture. Add the vinegar, water, spices, chipotle purée, sugar and some sea salt. Purée until very smooth. Pour into a saucepan and cook over medium–low heat for 10 minutes to bring the flavours together.

Preheat a barbecue or chargrill (griddle) pan to high. Rub the pork with the sugar and chilli powder and season. Barbecue for 3 minutes each side. Thickly slice the meat and serve with the red sauce. Top with the coriander and pickled onion.

PREP AHEAD

The sauce can be made 4 days ahead and refrigerated. It also freezes well.

THE SKINNY

The tasty sauce is made primarily from charred tomatoes and vegetables and is quite healthy. Pork tenderloin is a very lean meat.

Slow-roasted pork with spice crust and pomegranate glaze

preparation time 15 minutes / cooking time 3 hours / serves 6

Aromatic spices and pomegranate molasses make an exotic sauce for this slow-roasted pork. Neck is a particularly lean cut that has enough marbling to slowly melt away during the slow-cooking process resulting in flaky tender shreds of meat. You could make basmati rice boiled with Puy (tiny blue-green) lentils or jewelled couscous to serve alongside.

1 teaspoon olive oil
1.5 kg (3 lb 5 oz) piece of pork leg, shoulder or neck, trimmed of all fat
1 large onion, roughly chopped
1 teaspoon cumin seeds, roughly crushed
1 teaspoon coriander seeds, roughly crushed
1 teaspoon fennel seeds, roughly crushed
1 teaspoon chilli flakes
3 garlic cloves, smashed into a paste
400 ml (14 fl oz) water
75 ml (2⅛ fl oz) pomegranate molasses
fresh pomegranate seeds and chopped flat-leaf (Italian) parsley, to serve

Preheat the oven to 150°C (300°F/Gas 2).

Heat the olive oil in a non-stick frying pan over high heat. Season the pork well with sea salt and freshly ground black pepper, then sear on all sides until browned.

Place the onion in a large roasting tray. Mix all of the dry spices and garlic paste together with some sea salt and freshly ground black pepper in a small bowl. Rub this mixture all over the meat, then place the pork on top of the onion. Pour the water into the tray and cover tightly with foil. Roast for 2½ hours, then remove the foil. If the water has evaporated, add a bit more to the tray. Pour the pomegranate molasses over the pork and continue to roast, uncovered, for another 30 minutes or until the meat is tender and a sticky glaze has formed on top. Serve on a platter with the fresh pomegranate seeds and parsley scattered over.

PREP AHEAD

Marinate the meat in the spice mixture the day before and refrigerate.

THE SKINNY

Always trim off any obvious fat on the outside of the meat. The marbling on the inside will melt away during the slow cooking.

Mustard rack of lamb with dried cherry and shallot port sauce

preparation time 15 minutes / marinating time 1 hour / cooking time 25–35 minutes / serves 4

Although you would consider rack of lamb off limits for skinny cooking, once the layer of fat is taken off, it's not such a calorie crusher. The lean tender fillet beneath gets sealed in with fresh thyme and mustard while it roasts. The port gravy is a fitting sauce for this elegant cut of meat.

4 x three-cutlet racks of lamb, trimmed
   of most fat, and bones cleaned
2 garlic cloves, chopped
1 heaped tablespoon chopped thyme
2 tablespoons tawny or regular port
2 teaspoons olive oil
3 tablespoons Dijon mustard
crushed baby (new) potatoes
   or celeriac purée, to serve

Dried cherry and shallot port sauce

250 ml (9 fl oz/1 cup) tawny
   or regular port
2 tablespoons dried sour cherries,
   roughly chopped
2 teaspoons olive oil
2 French shallots (eschalots),
   finely chopped
1 tablespoon plain (all-purpose) flour
250 ml (9 fl oz/1 cup) beef stock
1 tablespoon redcurrant jelly

Season the racks of lamb with sea salt and freshly ground black pepper and place in a bowl with the garlic and half the thyme. Pour the port over and allow to marinate for 1 hour or more (up to overnight) if you have time.

Preheat the oven to 200°C (400°F/Gas 6). Drain the meat dry and season all over. Heat the olive oil in a frying pan over high heat until very hot and sear the lamb, fat side down, until golden. Place the lamb, fat side up, in a heavy-based flameproof roasting tray. Rub the mustard all over the lamb and sprinkle with more seasoning and the remaining thyme. Roast for 15 minutes for rare, 20 minutes for medium and 25 minutes for well-done. Transfer the lamb to a wire rack placed over a tray and cover loosely with foil to rest for 10 minutes. Reserve the roasting tray. The resting is important for perfect pink meat so do be sure to build in time to do this.

Meanwhile, make the dried cherry and shallot port sauce. Heat the port until boiling and add the cherries. Remove from the heat and allow to sit for 5 minutes.

Scrape out all the oil from the lamb roasting tray. Heat the olive oil in the roasting tray over medium heat, add the shallot and sauté for a few minutes or until just soft. Add the flour and stir for 1 minute over medium heat, then add the port mixture and stock. Simmer for 5 minutes or until the sauce thickens. Add the redcurrant jelly and season. Remove from the heat. Serve the lamb with the sauce and the crushed potatoes or celeriac purée.

PREP AHEAD

The lamb can be seared and the sauce can be made using the oil that the lamb was seared in. Roast the lamb just before you want to eat.

THE SKINNY

Although a tiny bit of the lamb dripping is used to make the sauce, it allows all the bits of flavour from the lamb to come through.

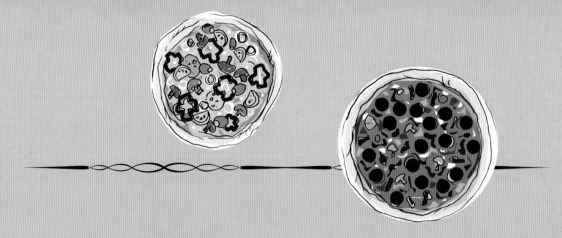

Mastering refrigerator pizza dough

Pizza doesn't have to be fattening. It all comes down to the cheese and meat toppings you choose. Just a little cheese tastes good but it doesn't need heaps of it. Same goes for the meat; a small taste is great but you don't need a lot. The dough, vegetables, meats and tomato sauce are all fairly skinny.

No one has time to make dough after work and then let it rise, so this method is perfect for a busy lifestyle. Using refrigerator dough, you can make it, refrigerate it for up to 3 days and just take out the portion you want 3 hours before using. It makes an inexpensive, healthy and fun dinner. The possibilities for variations are endless.

There are millions of different pizza dough recipes but they don't vary very much: yeast, water, flour, salt and olive oil. I prefer the Napoli-style pizza — bubbly soft with a crisp crust, not too thin and not too thick.

FLOUR Different varieties can produce an entirely different result. Strong bread or plain (all-purpose) flour makes a heavier dough and '00' (finely milled Italian flour) results in something softer.

OLIVE OIL If you like ultra-thin crisp pizza, then mixing olive oil into the dough will impart that brittle texture. Otherwise, use it to keep the dough moist while it rises.

YEAST Be sure to use dry active yeast not fast acting (which leaves little time to develop flavour). Only a small amount (¼ teaspoon per 500 grams) is required for slow-rising dough and it will give the pizza base more flavour and depth and create more air bubbles.

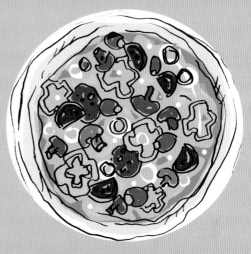

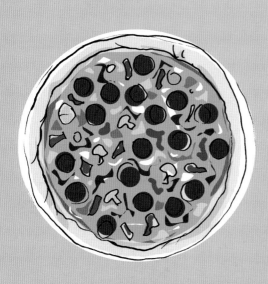

GETTING THE DOUGH RIGHT A light bubbly crisp dough comes down to this: soft light sticky dough equals an airy bubbly base; a heavy dry dough equals a solid heavy one. You want to aim for a slightly sticky light dough. But try not to get hung up on measuring, just add enough flour to the dough after the initial suggested amount so that you can mix or knead it together. After mixing it into a ball, oil your hands to work with it. Even if it's sticky (and it will be), persevere so you don't have to add too much flour. Using an electric mixer with a dough hook is a good option if you don't want to knead the dough by hand. It also allows you to work with a much stickier dough.

USE THE REFRIGERATOR TO RISE THE DOUGH The longer dough takes to rise, the more flavour it develops. Make sure the dough is oiled and covered in plastic wrap so it doesn't dry out and impede rising. When you want to use it over 3 days, take out the portion you need, let it come to room temperature, then make the pizzas.

PIZZA STONES Any oven can be used but using a pizza stone results in crisper pizza than using a baking tray. Put your pizza stone in a cold oven, then turn the temperature as high as it will go (stones need to go in a cold oven or they may crack).

PIZZA PEELS Although you can use a baking tray to take the pizza in and out of the oven, a pizza peel is best. Cover it with polenta, flour or semolina and place your dough over it. They will be the 'wheels' that allow the pizza to slide onto the stone.

Refrigerator pizza dough

preparation time 15 minutes / **rising time** 2–5 hours / **makes** six 25 cm (10 inch) diameter bases

500 g (1 lb 2 oz) oo flour,
   plus 3 tablespoons extra
1 teaspoon sea salt
400 ml (14 fl oz) warm water
¼ teaspoon dried active yeast
   (not fast acting)
olive oil, for greasing

Place the flour and salt in a large bowl or the bowl of an electric mixer. Fill a measuring jug with the warm water. It should be 'hand hot'; not so hot that you can't put your finger in but also not too lukewarm. Add the yeast, mix and wait about 5 minutes or so for little chunks to float up to the top. This is important because it means the yeast is working. Sometimes instant yeast can go off and it's infuriating to discover later. Always be sure and test it.

Fit the dough hook attachment to your mixer. Turn the motor on and slowly pour in the liquid. Knead until a dough forms. It should pull away completely at the base and come together as a ball. If it doesn't, slowly add up to 3 tablespoons of extra flour, a little at a time until it does. Continue kneading in the mixer for 5–7 minutes or until smooth and elastic.

Oil your hands, a bowl and a sheet of plastic wrap. Take out the dough, place in the bowl, oil the dough all over and cover with the oiled plastic. Place in the refrigerator for up to 3 days. (If you want to use the dough on the same day of making, skip the chilling and leave the dough to rise at room temperature until doubled in size.)

When you want to use it, take out the portion you want and let it double in size at room temperature. It should still be covered with plastic wrap and the surface of the dough should be oiled. The temperature of your kitchen will determine how quickly it rises. During the summer it may only take a couple of hours, but in winter, it may take 4–5 hours. If you have a cold draughty kitchen, then turn on the oven for 1 minute, turn off the heat, then place the bowl inside for the dough rise.

Pizza with Italian sausage, peperoncini and sweet onions

preparation time 15 minutes / cooking time 35 minutes / chilling time 30 minutes / serves 4–6

This is my all-time favourite pizza. I usually buy low-fat lean Italian sausages made with chicken or turkey and I don't use a huge quantity either. If buying the pork variety, then make sure the meat percentage is high. This makes six pizzas but if you only want to make four, then you can refrigerate the extra dough for up to 3 days or, even better, use it to make garlic flat bread or Middle Eastern lavash with spices. Freeze the extra sauce.

Pizza bases

1 quantity refrigerator pizza dough
    (see page 156), at room temperature
    and doubled in size
semolina flour or polenta, for dusting

Sauce

1 tablespoon olive oil
3 garlic cloves, thinly sliced
2 x 400 g (14 oz) tins whole roma
    (plum) tomatoes
1 tablespoon tomato paste
    (concentrated purée)
2 teaspoons dried oregano
1 teaspoon sea salt

Toppings

3 lean sausages (turkey or pork),
    casings removed and meat crumbled
olive oil spray
1 teaspoon fennel seeds
1 large pinch of chilli flakes
65 g (2⅛ oz/½ cup) grated low-fat
    mozzarella
thinly sliced peperoncini (Italian pickled
    peppers) or roasted marinated
    capsicum (pepper)
2 white or red onions, thinly sliced
1 tablespoon oregano leaves

To make the sauce. Heat the olive oil in a saucepan over high heat. Add the garlic and sauté until golden, about 3 minutes. Add the tomatoes and break up a bit with a spoon. Add the tomato paste. Sprinkle in the dried oregano and salt. Simmer until all the liquid has evaporated and the sauce has thickened nicely, about 20–25 minutes. Scrape into a bowl, cool, then refrigerate until chilled. (It works best to make pizzas with cold sauce.)

If you have a pizza stone, place it on the lowest rack of your oven. Turn your oven up to the highest temperature it will go.

To prepare the sausage ready for topping, heat a non-stick frying pan sprayed with a tiny bit of olive oil over high heat. Add the sausage meat, fennel seeds and chilli flakes and cook until it has browned a bit, breaking up the meat with a spoon. Remove from the heat.

To make the pizza bases, knock back the dough and divide into 6 pieces. Working with 1 piece at a time, roll out each piece on a lightly floured surface with a rolling pin to make a 25 cm (10 inch) diameter round, about 5 mm thick. Spread a teaspoon or so of the semolina on the pizza peel (or you can use a baking tray without a rim). Place the pizza base on top and make sure it can move around. Spread a thin layer of the sauce over the pizza base, scatter over a little cheese, some sausage, a small handful of peperoncini and onion and finish with a sprinkle of oregano leaves. Slide the pizza onto the preheated pizza stone and cook for 4–5 minutes or until the base is crisp. Enjoy your pizza straight out of the oven, then make the next — that's part of the fun of homemade pizzas.

If you want to cook your pizzas all at once, then pan pizzas are the solution. You will need two large baking trays with a rim — the ones I use are 36 cm x 26 cm (14¼ inch x 10½ inch) with a 2 cm (¾ inch) lip. Sprinkle the trays with semolina. Take 4 portions of dough (you will need to save the remaining 2 portions of dough) and use 2 portions for each tray. Roll out to 1 cm (½ inch) thick and place on the trays. Add the sauce and toppings and bake in a preheated 220°C (425°F/ Gas 7) oven for 12–15 minutes or until the crust is golden. (Serves 4.)

OTHER GREAT COMBINATIONS

Spinach, jamón and feta

Grilled eggplant (aubergine), garlic and pecorino

Thinly sliced white onion, tomatoes, fresh oregano and low-fat mozzarella

Mushroom, asiago cheese, garlic and chilli flakes

Tomatoes, goat's cheese and pancetta

Fresh figs, pancetta and a small amount of Gorgonzola or low-fat mozzarella

Thin base of pesto, chicken, red onion and low-fat mozzarella

Smoky Spanish beef stew with cannellini beans

preparation time 15 minutes / cooking time 1¼ hours / serves 6

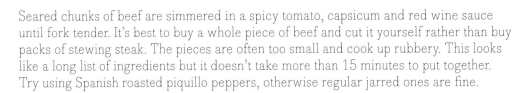

Seared chunks of beef are simmered in a spicy tomato, capsicum and red wine sauce until fork tender. It's best to buy a whole piece of beef and cut it yourself rather than buy packs of stewing steak. The pieces are often too small and cook up rubbery. This looks like a long list of ingredients but it doesn't take more than 15 minutes to put together. Try using Spanish roasted piquillo peppers, otherwise regular jarred ones are fine.

2 roasted red capsicums (peppers)
2 tablespoons olive oil
800 g (1 lb 12 oz) beef (stewing cut),
   cut into 5 cm (2 inch) chunks
1 large brown onion, chopped
2 garlic cloves, chopped
2 tablespoons smoked paprika
250 ml (9 fl oz/1 cup) red wine
2 tablespoons sherry vinegar
2 tablespoons honey
15 small carrots, scrubbed and trimmed
400 ml (14 fl oz) tomato passata
   (puréed tomatoes)
2 x 400 g (14 oz) tins cannellini
   (white) beans, drained
chopped flat-leaf (Italian) parsley,
   to serve

If you're not using jarred roasted capsicums and you want to roast your own, place the capsicums on a baking tray and cook under a hot grill (broiler), turning occasionally, until blackened and blistered all over. Alternatively, place the capsicums directly on top of a low gas flame and turn frequently until blackened. Transfer to a bowl, cover with plastic wrap and allow to cool. Peel and remove the seeds but do not wash the flesh.

Place the roasted capsicum in a food processor with any juices and purée until smooth.

Heat 1 tablespoon of the olive oil in a large heavy-based saucepan over high heat. Season the beef with sea salt and freshly ground black pepper and brown in batches. Remove from the pan and set aside.

Reduce the heat to medium, add the onion, garlic and remaining olive oil to the same pan, season and sauté for 6–8 minutes or until softened. Add the paprika, roasted capsicum purée, wine, vinegar, honey, carrots and tomato passata. Cover with a lid and cook over low heat for 1 hour or until the beef is fork tender. Just as the beef is ready, add the beans and warm through. Taste for seasoning. Serve with a sprinkling of parsley.

PREP AHEAD

The stew can be made 2–3 days ahead and refrigerated or frozen.

THE SKINNY

Stews such as this are low in fat as most of the sauce is just tasty tomatoes and wine. The beans and carrots make it a one-pot dish.

Chicken, apricot and tomato tagine

preparation time 15 minutes / cooking time 50 minutes / serves 6

When my family and I visited Morocco a couple of years ago, I was surprised at how rustic the tagines were. Night after night, eating out at restaurants, the same trio of carrot, lamb on the bone and onions appeared. It was nothing like the exotic spice-aromatic stews I had read about and cooked. A friend told me later that you need to be invited to someone's house in order to get the dishes one reads about. Not having that luxury at my disposal I decided to carry on with my own interpretations and this is one of my favourites. Serve some couscous mixed with herbs alongside.

2 teaspoons olive oil

12 small skinless chicken thigh fillets,
    trimmed of all fat, halved

2 brown onions, thinly sliced

5 cm (2 inch) piece of ginger,
    finely shredded

3 garlic cloves, finely chopped

1 teaspoon saffron threads

1 teaspoon boiling water

1 teaspoon ground ginger

1 teaspoon ground cumin

1 large cinnamon stick

2 tablespoons tomato paste
    (concentrated purée)

500 ml (17 fl oz/2 cups) chicken stock

12 plump dried apricots, cut into
    quarters

2 tablespoons honey

juice of 1½ lemons, plus lemon wedges
    to serve

finely chopped coriander (cilantro)
    and steamed couscous, to serve

Heat 1 teaspoon of the olive oil over high heat in a large saucepan. Season the chicken well with sea salt and freshly ground black pepper and sear until browned on both sides. Remove from the pan and set aside.

Add the remaining oil to the pan, along with the onion, ginger, garlic and some salt and pepper to taste. Sauté for 10 minutes or until the onion has softened. Slightly crush the saffron, pour over the boiling water and allow to infuse for a minute. Add the saffron mixture and all of the spices to the pan and cook for 1 minute or until aromatic. Add the tomato paste, stock, apricots, honey, lemon juice and chicken. Cook over medium–low heat for 30 minutes or until the chicken is tender. Sprinkle with the coriander and serve with the lemon wedges and couscous.

PREP AHEAD

The tagine can be made 2 days ahead and refrigerated or frozen. Gently reheat in a saucepan and add a little stock or water if it's too thick.

THE SKINNY

Tagine sauces are comprised of mainly spice, onion and stock, making them very healthy choices as well as gorgeous meals.

Hainanese chicken with sweet soy and chilli dipping sauce

preparation time 15 minutes / **cooking time** 10 minutes / **standing time** 1 hour / serves 4

This Malaysian dish originated in China but is now eaten by both cultures. A whole chicken is poached and then eaten with garlic rice, cucumber and a sweet soy and ginger-spiked sauce. The meat poaches beautifully white and retains its juices. It's important you use the right size chicken for this. If it's bigger than 1.2 kilograms, then up the initial boiling time to 15 minutes instead of 10 minutes.

2 litres (70 fl oz) water

1 x 1.2 kg (2 lb 10 oz) whole chicken (preferably free-range)

2 teaspoons vegetable oil

2 garlic cloves, finely chopped

200 g (7 oz/1 cup) basmati or long-grain rice

2 Lebanese (short) cucumbers, shaved into ribbons with a vegetable peeler

1 small handful coriander (cilantro) leaves, roughly chopped

Sweet soy and chilli dipping sauce

1 thumb-sized red chilli, seeds removed and chopped

½ garlic clove, chopped

1 cm (½ inch) piece of ginger, finely chopped

1½ tablespoons sweet soy sauce (kecap manis), or 3 tablespoons regular soy sauce mixed with 1 tablespoon soft brown sugar

2 teaspoons rice vinegar

2 teaspoons caster (superfine) sugar

Bring the water to the boil in a large stockpot. Add the chicken (it should be covered completely with water) and simmer gently for 10 minutes. Turn off the heat but leave the pot on the stove and cover with a lid. Leave to sit for 1 hour.

Meanwhile, make the sweet soy and chilli dipping sauce. (If you don't want to chop all the ingredients by hand, you could pulse them in the food processor.) Combine all of the ingredients in a small bowl. Set aside.

About 10 minutes before the chicken is done, heat the vegetable oil in a saucepan over medium heat, add the garlic and sauté until golden. Add the rice and stir for 1 minute. Ladle in enough of the chicken-poaching liquid to cover the rice by 1 cm (½ inch). Cover with a lid, reduce the heat to low and cook for 8–10 minutes or until al dente.

Remove the chicken from the pot. Remove and discard the skin and chop the meat into pieces (see Note). Arrange the chicken on a platter with the cucumber and coriander. Serve with the rice and dipping sauce.

NOTE You can reserve the poaching liquid and bones and simmer for 1 hour with a chopped onion, carrot and celery stalk to make a delicious stock.

PREP AHEAD

The dipping sauce can be made on the morning of serving but everything else should be done 1–2 hours before eating.

THE SKINNY

Poaching chicken is a beautiful method for low-fat cooking and delicious juicy meat.

Skinny Puds

Pineapple and mint granita

preparation time 30 minutes / **freezing time** 3 hours / **makes** 1.5 litres (52 fl oz)

Granita is brilliant because you don't need an ice-cream machine. The fruit purée and sugar syrup are poured into a shallow pan and scraped three times during the freezing process. The result is granular pieces of fruity ice. This makes a big granita but if you are going to the trouble to make it, you may as well make a big batch. Baby pineapples are sweeter than the bigger versions and the fresh mint is a refreshing counterpart.

300 ml (10⅛ fl oz) water
250 g (9 oz) caster (superfine) sugar
1 kg (2 lb 4 oz) chopped pineapple flesh
4 tablespoons lime juice
1 large handful mint leaves,
    finely chopped
tropical fruit, such as mango or papaya,
    chopped, to serve

Bring the water and sugar to the boil and simmer for 5 minutes or until slightly syrupy. Allow to cool completely.

Purée the pineapple in a food processor, then push through a fine sieve to create a smooth purée. Discard any pulp in the sieve. Mix the cooled syrup, lime juice and mint with the purée. Pour into a shallow metal or glass tray (about 33 cm x 23 cm/13 inch x 9 inch) and place in the freezer.

After 2 hours, scrape the mixture with a fork. When breaking up the ice crystals, make long scrapes, raking the fork down the mixture repeatedly. Avoid mixing it up, which will result in a smooth texture more like sorbet. Freeze again for another 30 minutes, then repeat scraping and freezing two more times until grainy crystals have formed.

Serve with the tropical fruit.

PREP AHEAD

This will keep for 2 weeks in the freezer in an airtight container.

THE SKINNY

A clever way to get a good quota of fruit into you. Granted, it has a bit of sugar but it's still pretty healthy.

Little cocoa kisses

preparation time 10 minutes / **cooking time** 1 hour / **makes** 60 tiny bites (depends on how big you make them)

These petite meringues are the powdery type and are quite easy to make. If you can make them last, they're quite a handy sweet snack. You can spoon them onto the baking tray, or do as I do and pipe them: fill a large zip-lock plastic bag with the mixture and snip off a corner with scissors. I like to pipe them small with a little curl at the top. Meringues have a few simple rules for success and, if you follow them, you won't run into problems. First start with a very clean bowl — grease will chemically react with the eggwhites and inhibit volume. Next, don't allow any yolk to get into the whites because any protein will, again, cause the whites to become foamy instead of glossy. Older eggs (2 weeks or so) work better than fresh ones and the most important consideration of all is that the whites need to be at room temperature.

2 large eggwhites, at room temperature
125 g (4½ oz) caster (superfine) sugar
1 teaspoon cocoa powder
½ teaspoon vanilla extract

Preheat the oven to 120°C (235°F/Gas ½). Line two baking trays with baking paper.

Place the eggwhite in the bowl of an electric mixer and beat with a tiny pinch of salt for 1–2 minutes or until soft peaks form. Add the sugar a tablespoonful at a time until incorporated. Keep whisking for 1–2 minutes or until stiff glossy peaks form, another minute or two. Sift the cocoa over, add the vanilla extract and gently fold through the mixture.

Spoon or pipe heaped teaspoons onto the baking trays. Bake for 1 hour. Remove and allow to cool on the trays. Store in an airtight container.

PREP AHEAD

The kisses can be made 3 days ahead and stored in an airtight container.

THE SKINNY

With only sugar and a tiny bit of cocoa, these are an ideal skinny treat with almost no fat. It's good to have something like this around when you get a sweet craving instead of eating something much worse.

Chewy meringues with blackberries and Greek yoghurt

preparation time 20 minutes / cooking time 35 minutes / cooling time 2 hours / makes 16

Meringues can be prepared in many ways. If you cook them on low heat for hours, they become powdery; if cooked with a combination of high and low, you get a chewy toffee centre with a crisp exterior. These are the latter, which are nice on their own or as a full-on dessert.

150 ml (5⅛ fl oz) eggwhite (from about 4 eggs), at room temperature
200 g (7 oz) caster (superfine) sugar
2 teaspoons cornflour (cornstarch)
1 teaspoon white vinegar
300 g (10½ oz) blackberries or other berries
1½ tablespoons icing (confectioners') sugar
250 g (9 oz) low-fat Greek yoghurt
tiny mint leaves, for garnishing

Preheat the oven to 150°C (300°F/Gas 2). Line two large baking trays with baking paper.

Place the eggwhite in the bowl of an electric mixer and beat until soft peaks form. Add the caster sugar a tablespoonful at a time until incorporated. Keep whisking for 1–2 minutes or until stiff glossy peaks form. Sift the cornflour over, add the vinegar and gently fold through the mixture.

Place 16 dollops of meringue, about 7.5–10 cm (3–4 inches) in size, leaving plenty of space in between. Reduce the oven to 120°C (235°F/Gas ½) and bake for 35 minutes. Turn the oven off and allow the meringues to cool for a couple of hours. This is an important step because if you take them out at this point, they will be soft; the cooling process makes them crisp.

To serve, gently crush the berries in a bowl with the back of a fork and mix in the icing sugar until dissolved. Serve the meringues with the berries and yoghurt, garnished with the mint.

PREP AHEAD

These will keep for 4–5 days in an airtight container.

THE SKINNY

Although meringues have a lot of sugar, they don't have any egg yolks or butter. The low-fat Greek yoghurt also replaces fat-laden whipped cream.

Caramelised grilled mango with mint

preparation time 10 minutes / cooking time 5 minutes / serves 4

This low-effort dessert works well with tropical fruit, such as mangoes or pineapple slices. It's the perfect ending to complement an Asian meal. Vanilla paste, which is a little pot of scraped seeds, is sold in most supermarkets. It allows you to use a little without much waste.

2 large ripe but firm mangoes
½ teaspoon vanilla paste (or ½ vanilla
    bean, split and seeds scraped)
3 tablespoons caster (superfine) sugar
frozen yoghurt or low-fat raspberry
    sorbet and mint leaves, to serve

Slice the cheeks off the mangoes. Lightly score a criss-cross pattern on the cut sides. Add the vanilla paste or seeds to the sugar. Mix well and spread across the mangoes. Place under a hot grill (broiler) and cook for 3–4 minutes or until the sugar caramelises. Remove and serve in bowls with a scoop of frozen yoghurt or sorbet with the mint leaves scattered over.

PREP AHEAD

The vanilla sugar can be made a couple of days ahead and stored in an airtight container. The mangoes are best grilled just before serving.

THE SKINNY

Fresh vanilla seeds give fruit a luxurious tropical boost. Frozen yoghurt or sorbet is a low-calorie partner for fruit, and you won't feel like you've missed out on a sweet ending.

Rhubarb and strawberry compote

preparation time 5 minutes / cooking time 15 minutes / serves 4

This makes a great pudding with low-fat fromage frais or Greek yoghurt, or use it as a topping for chewy meringues with blackberries and Greek yoghurt (see page 170). The strawberries' sweetness foils the rhubarb's sharp edge.

400 g (14 oz) thin rhubarb, leaves trimmed, stalks cut into 5 cm (2 inch) lengths
150 g (5¼ oz) strawberries, hulled and halved
2 tablespoons caster (superfine) sugar
2 tablespoons orange juice
1 vanilla bean, split and seeds scraped
low-fat fromage frais or Greek yoghurt, to serve

Preheat the oven to 190°C (375°F/Gas 5).

Place the rhubarb and strawberries in a large shallow baking dish. Sprinkle the sugar over and drizzle over the orange juice. Add the vanilla seeds and mix well to distribute. Roast for 15 minutes or until just tender.

Serve warm with the fromage frais or yoghurt.

PREP AHEAD

The rhubarb should be roasted shortly before serving. You can chop it 2 hours before but don't mix it until just before roasting.

THE SKINNY

Warm compotes are comforting sweets in the winter and amazingly healthy.

Little elderflower sparkling berry jellies

preparation time 15 minutes / *setting time* 5 hours / *serves* 6

Jello or jelly, depending on what country you're in, has moved on from the days of lurid-coloured moulded shapes made from powdered mixes. It's not difficult to make your own jelly using gelatine sheets or powder and flavoured juice, wine or cordial. It's particularly refreshing in the summer and a wonderful vehicle for fresh berries and other fruit. Elderflower cordial, the quintessential English drink, is made from crushed elderflowers, lemon and sugar. Its perfumed scent is concentrated and meant to be mixed with water, one part to ten, so only a small amount is needed here.

6 gold-strength gelatine leaves
150 ml (5 fl oz) elderflower cordial
100 g (3½ oz/⅔ cup) caster
   (superfine) sugar
500 ml (17 fl oz/2 cups) Champagne
   or sparkling white wine
250 g (9 oz) mixed berries, such as
   halved strawberries, blueberries
   or blackberries
low-fat Greek yoghurt, to serve

Soak the gelatine leaves in cold water until soft, about 5 minutes.

Heat the elderflower cordial with the sugar in a saucepan over low heat for 5 minutes or until the sugar has dissolved.

Drain the gelatine, discarding the water and squeeze out the excess water with your hands.

Add to the warm cordial mixture and stir over low heat until the gelatine has dissolved. Don't allow to boil but just keep at a low simmer. Remove from the heat and allow to cool a bit.

Pour in the Champagne and mix. Divide the berries between six dariole moulds (ramekins), small teacups or any small container that is at least 200 ml (7 fl oz) capacity. Pour half of the liquid mixture in and refrigerate for 1 hour.

Remove from the refrigerator and pour the remaining liquids into the moulds. This two-step process will keep the berries in the middle of the mixture instead of them floating to the top. Refrigerate again for another 4 hours or until firmly set.

If using dariole moulds, to unmould them, quickly dip the mould into just-boiled water, then invert onto a plate. The jelly will slip out but if it doesn't, dip it again and repeat.

Serve with the low-fat Greek yoghurt or just on its own.

PREP AHEAD

The jellies can be prepared 2 days ahead and stored in the refrigerator.

THE SKINNY

The floral tasting elderflower allows for less sugar and the berries keep it bright and healthy.

Baked apples stuffed with dates, cinnamon and oats

preparation time 10 minutes / cooking time 40 minutes / serves 4

For a light dessert, these baked apples are quite decadent. Cinnamon-spiced oats mixed with dates, lemon zest and dark brown sugar create a crisp topping without large amounts of butter. The sweet wine keeps the apple flesh soft and turns into a lovely sauce. Top with vanilla frozen yoghurt or a small spoonful of dulce de leche sauce.

4 apples (such as delicious, cox
   or bramley)
finely grated zest of 1 lemon and
   juice of ½ lemon
10 g (¼ oz) unsalted butter,
   at room temperature
60 g (2¼ oz) soft brown sugar
2 large fresh dates, pitted
   and finely chopped
1 tablespoon plain (all-purpose) flour
2 teaspoons ground cinnamon
2 tablespoons rolled oats
170 ml (5½ fl oz/⅔ cup) Sauternes,
   muscat or other dessert wine
2 tablespoons flaked almonds
frozen vanilla yoghurt or
   dulce de leche sauce, to serve
   (optional)

Preheat the oven to 190°C (375°F/Gas 5). Cut the apples in half widthways and remove the core with a melon baller. Rub the cut sides with the lemon juice. In a small bowl, mix together the butter, sugar, dates, flour, cinnamon, oats and lemon zest. Divide between the apple halves, stuffing the mixture inside the cavity of each. Nestle the apple halves into a square baking dish that fits them snugly. Pour in the wine, scatter over the almonds, cover with foil and bake for 20 minutes. Remove the foil and bake for another 20 minutes or until the apples are tender, golden and crisp.

Serve on their own, with the frozen yoghurt or a drizzle of duche de leche sauce.

PREP AHEAD

The apples can be filled 4 hours ahead but rub well with lemon juice to prevent them from browning.

THE SKINNY

The dates keep the amount of sugar and butter down, while adding sweetness and texture. A tiny drizzle of dulce de leche is okay — it's made from sugar and milk but, unlike caramel sauce, there is no butter.

Frozen passionfruit yoghurt ice-cream

preparation time 10 minutes / cooling time 1 hour / freezing time 5 hours / makes 1 litre (35 fl oz/4 cups)

Once you make this, you will never buy frozen yoghurt again. It's so easy, delicious and best of all, fat-free! You will need to use thick Greek yoghurt to make this. I experimented with both the low-fat variety (98% fat-free) as well as the fat-free and you will be glad to know there wasn't any difference in texture or taste. If you don't have access to the thick Greek variety, then place plain low-fat yoghurt in a fine sieve and leave for 1 day in the refrigerator. The remaining thick mixture is the same as thick Greek yoghurt but you will most likely need 1 litre (35 fl oz/4 cups) if making your own. Any flavour fruit can be substituted in place of the passionfruit.

12 passionfruit
150 g (5½ oz/⅔ cup) caster
  (superfine) sugar
750 g (1 lb 10 oz) non-fat Greek yoghurt
1 vanilla bean, split and seeds scraped

Halve the passionfruit and scoop out the pulp. Strain the pulp through a fine sieve, reserving the juice and 2 tablespoons of the seeds. You will need 150 ml (5 fl oz) of juice. Heat the juice with the sugar and simmer for 5 minutes or until slightly syrupy. Mix the yoghurt, vanilla seeds and passionfruit syrup in a bowl. Place in the refrigerator for 2 hours, then churn in an ice-cream machine according to the manufacturer's instructions until thick, then add the reserved seeds. Freeze in a covered container until firm.

NOTE To make strawberry or raspberry frozen yoghurt, purée 400 g (14 oz) of your chosen fruit in a food processor, then push through a fine sieve. Discard the solids and mix the purée with the sugar and vanilla. Stir to dissolve, then mix into the yoghurt. Chopped bits of extra fruit can be mixed in when it has finished churning.

PREP AHEAD

The frozen yoghurt will keep for up to 1 month in the freezer.

THE SKINNY

Made with fat-free yoghurt, this is the skinniest iced treat you can make so enjoy! Unlike ice-cream, there are no eggs or cream.

Raspberry sorbet

preparation time 10 minutes / cooking time 7 minutes / chilling time 1 hour 20 minutes / freezing time 3 hours / makes 1 litre (35 fl oz/4 cups)

There is no better way to put punnets of summer fruit to good use than making sorbet. I've included a little liquid glucose syrup (available in the baking aisle in supermarkets). Without it, homemade sorbet can be a bit grainy so put in a few tablespoons to keep it velvety smooth. If you don't have an ice-cream machine, then you can make a granita instead (see pineapple and mint granita on page 168 for technique).

200 ml (7 fl oz) water
250 g (9 oz) caster (superfine) sugar
3 tablespoons liquid glucose
500 g (1 lb 2 oz) fresh or frozen
   raspberries
1 tablespoon lemon juice
fresh fruit, to serve

Bring the water, sugar and glucose syrup to the boil in a small saucepan over medium–high heat, then cook for 5–7 minutes or until it is a thin syrup. Pour into a bowl and allow to cool, then refrigerate for 20 minutes or until chilled.

Meanwhile, mash the raspberries with the lemon juice, then push through a fine sieve and discard the seeds.

Stir the purée into the cold syrup. Return to the fridge and chill for another 1 hour. Churn in an ice-cream machine according to the manufacturer's instructions until thick, then freeze in an airtight container.

Serve with fresh berries, chopped pineapple or mango.

PREP AHEAD

The sorbet can be frozen for up to 1 month.

THE SKINNY

Sorbet makes a perfect sweet treat, instead of ice-cream, and this one is packed with fruit.

Roasted plums with star anise and cinnamon

preparation time 10 minutes / cooking time 20 minutes / serves 4

Aromatic spices, vanilla and orange juice flavour these baked plums for an exotic warm fruit dessert. Serve with frozen mango sorbet or Greek yoghurt for a treat after Middle Eastern or Asian food.

6 small–medium red plums, halved
3 star anise
2 cinnamon sticks
juice of 2 large oranges
2 tablespoons honey
2 tablespoons soft brown sugar
1 teaspoon vanilla paste or ½ vanilla
    bean, split and seeds scraped
low-fat mango sorbet or Greek
    yoghurt, to serve

Preheat the oven to 180°C (350°F/Gas 4). Place the plums, cut side up, in a baking dish in one layer. Mix the remaining ingredients except the sorbet in a small bowl to combine. Pour over the fruit and bake for 20 minutes or until golden and bubbling. Serve with the sorbet or yoghurt.

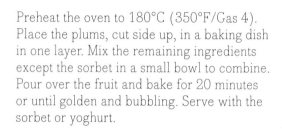

PREP AHEAD

The plums can be baked for three-quarters of the cooking time, then finished off just before serving.

THE SKINNY

With the exception of sugar, there isn't anything else too high on calories in this pudding.

Peach Melba

preparation time 10 minutes / cooking time 10 minutes / serves 4

The scarlet raspberry sauce and bright orange peaches are a feast for your eyes as well as your stomach. Stone fruit takes on a silky character when poached and there is no better way to prepare summer's bounty. It's important to use good tasting ripe fruit for this. If your peaches are hard, let them ripen at room temperature for a few days before using.

500 ml (17 fl oz/2 cups) water
110 g (3¾ oz/½ cup) caster (superfine) sugar
4 freestone (slipstone) peaches, ripe but not too soft
250 g (9 oz) fresh or frozen raspberries
low-fat frozen yoghurt, to serve
mint leaves, to garnish

Combine the water and 75 g (2⅔ oz/⅓ cup) of the sugar in a saucepan over low heat and stir until the sugar dissolves.

Score the base of each peach. Increase the heat to medium, add the peaches and poach for 10 minutes. Remove from the liquid, and peel with your hands. Halve and remove the stones. If you find this tricky, as sometimes the stones stick a little, hold the fruit between paper towel, pull and firmly twist.

Mash the raspberries with the remaining sugar, then push through a fine sieve and discard the seeds.

Arrange the peaches in dessert bowls and spoon the raspberry sauce over each. Top with a scoop of the frozen yoghurt and the mint leaves.

PREP AHEAD

The peaches can be poached and peeled the day before but store in the poaching syrup in the refrigerator until needed. The raspberry sauce can also be made 1 day ahead.

THE SKINNY

Normally this would be served with ice-cream but frozen yoghurt won't leave you lacking anything. The fruit and sauce are fat-free and very low in sugar as well.

Apple and pear chips with cinnamon and lemon sugar

preparation time 10 minutes / cooking time 45 minutes / **makes** about 60 rings

It sounds quite earnest to say you're going to make your own dried fruit, but once you see how easy and cheap it is, you'll be hooked. Try other fruits such as pineapple, sliced strawberries or raspberries. You will need a mandolin (inexpensive plastic ones are easy to get hold of and work very well).

2 granny smith apples
2 firm pears (comice, bartlett or any bigger variety)
juice of 1 lemon
2 tablespoons icing (confectioners') sugar

Preheat the oven to 100°C (200°F/Gas ½). Line two baking trays with silicone baking mats or baking paper. Use a mandolin to slice the fruit into 3 mm (⅛ inch) thick slices, going all the way through the core and place in a large bowl. Add the lemon juice, then sprinkle over the sugar. Gently toss to combine, being careful they don't break. Place on the baking trays in a single layer. Bake for 45 minutes or until they are chewy and fairly dry (the pears may take up to 20 minutes longer depending on what variety you use). Remove from the oven and peel them from the tray so they don't stick. Cool on a wire rack, then store immediately in an airtight container.

PREP AHEAD

These will keep for 3 days in an airtight container.

THE SKINNY

Low in fat and a perfect sweet snack. Pack them in your handbag or work lunchbox so you're not tempted with other more 'dangerous' nibbles lurking in the vending machines.

Skinny tangerine dreamsicle lollies

preparation time 10 minutes / cooking time 15 minutes / freezing time 2 hours / serves 6

As a child, my favourite popsicle (or lollie as we call it in Britain) was tangerine dreamsicle. It's vanilla ice-cream coated in an intense tangerine sorbet. This skinny interpretation is very close in taste to it and doesn't take more than 10 minutes to make.

600 ml (21 fl oz) freshly squeezed
   tangerine or orange juice
100 g (3½ oz) caster (superfine) sugar
200 g (7 oz/¾ cup) low-fat Greek
   yoghurt

Combine the juice and 75 g (2⅔ oz/⅓ cup) of the sugar in a saucepan and stir over medium heat until the sugar dissolves. Simmer for 15 minutes or until reduced by half. Cool to room temperature.

Combine the yoghurt and remaining sugar. Divide half of the juice mixture among six 100 ml (3½ fl oz) capacity popsicle moulds. Top with the yoghurt, then pour in the remaining juice mixture. Freeze for 2 hours or until firm.

PREP AHEAD

The popsicles can be frozen for up to 1 month.

THE SKINNY

Enjoy an icy skinny treat that tastes like ice-cream with low sugar and hardly any fat.

Chianti and anise poached pears

preparation time 10 minutes / cooking time 30 minutes / serves 4

Anise seed has a liquorice taste very similar to fennel but sweeter. When added to red wine with vanilla seeds it makes an exquisite poaching elixir for pears. My favourite type of pears are comice, with sweet flesh and big chubby bottoms, but other varieties can be used. Be sure to use a small saucepan that keeps the pears snug while poaching.

1 x 750 ml (26 fl oz/3 cups) Chianti
   or other Italian red wine
200 g (7 oz) caster (superfine) sugar
1 large strip orange peel
1 large strip lemon peel
1 teaspoon anise seeds or fennel seeds
1 vanilla bean, split and seeds scraped
4 comice or other large firm pears,
   peeled
Greek yoghurt or low-fat crème fraîche,
   to serve

Bring the wine, sugar, citrus peels, anise seeds and vanilla bean and seeds to the boil in a large saucepan. Reduce the heat to a low simmer and add the pears. Cook for 20–25 minutes or until the pears can easily be pierced with a skewer. The cooking time will vary slightly depending on the size of the pears. Use a slotted spoon to transfer the pears to a deep-sided dish, just large enough to hold the pears. Keep warm.

Strain the poaching liquid and pour it back into the pan. Cook over medium–high heat for 5 minutes or until reduced and slightly syrupy. Pour over the pears.

To serve, place a pear in a shallow bowl with 2 generous tablespoons of the syrup spooned over. A dollop of Greek yoghurt or low-fat crème fraîche is also delicious eaten alongside.

PREP AHEAD

The pears can be poached and stored in their poaching liquid in the refrigerator overnight. Gently reheat the pears in their liquid, then remove the pears and reduce the sauce into a syrup.

THE SKINNY

The red wine and spiced poaching liquid gives the pears a spicy depth and turns this dessert into a sticky skinny syrup to pour over the pears.

Lemon angel food cake

preparation time 15 minutes / cooking time 30 minutes / serves 8

It's unfathomable to think there is a cake out there that isn't fattening. Angel food, a very popular American cake, is similar to the classic sponge but doesn't have any egg yolks. The whipped eggwhite makes it light as a cloud and it is delicious with fresh berries or even a little drizzle of icing sugar mixed with water. For a skinny trifle, layer leftover chunks of cake with berry coulis and Greek yoghurt.

360 ml (12¼ fl oz) eggwhite (from about 10 eggs), at room temperature
1½ teaspoons cream of tartar
250 g (9 oz) caster (superfine) sugar
2 tablespoons finely grated lemon zest
1 teaspoon vanilla extract
125 g (4½ oz) cake (superfine) flour or 'oo' flour
berry or passionfruit coulis or low-fat Greek yoghurt and fresh fruit, to serve

Preheat the oven to 180°C (350°F/Gas 4). Place the eggwhite in the bowl of an electric mixer and beat on medium speed until frothy, then add the cream of tartar. Increase the speed to high and, when the whites start getting fluffy, slowly spoon in the sugar until all of it is incorporated and stiff glossy peaks form. Fold in the zest and vanilla.

Remove the bowl from the mixer. Using a large metal spoon, sift one-third of the flour over the mixture and fold through. Be gentle but quick so the whites don't deflate. Add the remaining flour in two more batches, then pour into an ungreased 25 cm (10 inch) round angel food cake tin (tube cake tin or non-fluted Bundt cake tin). Run a knife through the batter to make sure there aren't big air pockets.

Bake on the centre oven rack for 30 minutes or until a skewer comes out clean. Remove from the oven and turn the pan upside down on the counter. This is important otherwise the cake will deflate. Allow to cool completely, about 2 hours.

Run a knife around the side and base to remove the cake from the tin. Serve with your choice of accompaniments.

PREP AHEAD

The cake will keep covered for a couple of days.

THE SKINNY

With the exception of the sugar, this is a pretty healthy sweet. If you're craving a slice of cake, this is completely guilt-free.

Acknowledgements

This book wouldn't have been possible without the help of so many people. It all started with Kay Scarlett, who commissioned this to follow *Meals in Heels*. You are a class act and left some big shoes to fill. The time I had to work with you will always be cherished.

Kylie Walker, I am very thankful to you picking up the reins on this project, being so supportive and making room for the photographs in the budget.

Emilia Toia, your masterful eye for design and sharp ideas are so impressive. Yet again, you've taken my recipes and created a jaw-dropping book.

Gabriella Sterio, your attention to detail and careful management of this have not gone unnoticed. Thank you for putting so much hard work in with such a positive attitude. Even though we were halfway across the world from each other, I always felt confident everything was swimming along. You are an amazing editor.

Belinda So, I knew I was in safe hands with you on the job, editing my text. The tiniest of details never miss your eyes and you really understand what I'm trying to do. It meant a lot to me to have you working on this after *Meals in Heels*.

Maja Smend, your photos are beautiful and I always enjoy food styling with you. You're not afraid to push the boundaries and get the perfect photograph.

Kathy Kordalis and Donna Laveran, thank you so much for all of your help testing recipes. Your chopping, washing up and suggestions were so appreciated. It was more fun than work.

Sarah Birks, thank you for pulling my props together with your eagle eye for design and good taste. It was you who cemented the idea for this book in my head. I always love working with you.

Megan Hess, your illustrations are gorgeous and oh so glamorous. Thanks, once again, for contributing such lovely work.

Christine Osmond and Murdoch test kitchen, I can sleep at night knowing you have been through the recipes in here with a fine tooth comb. I feel very fortunate to have such a resource like you for my book.

Pat, Liam and Riley, I couldn't have done this book without your voracious appetites, love and support. Thank God you're always up for something new.

Published in 2011 by Murdoch Books Pty Limited

Murdoch Books Australia
Pier 8/9
23 Hickson Road
Millers Point NSW 2000
Phone: +61 (0) 2 8220 2000
Fax: +61 (0) 2 8220 2558
www.murdochbooks.com.au
info@murdochbooks.com.au

Murdoch Books UK Limited
Erico House, 6th Floor
93–99 Upper Richmond Road
Putney, London SW15 2TG
Phone: +44 (0) 20 8785 5995
Fax: +44 (0) 20 8785 5985
www.murdochbooks.co.uk
info@murdochbooks.co.uk

For Corporate Orders & Custom Publishing contact
Noel Hammond, National Business Development Manager

Publisher: Kylie Walker
Design and concept: Emilia Toia
Illustrator: Megan Hess
Photographer: Maja Smend
Stylist: Jennifer Joyce
Project Editor: Gabriella Sterio
Editor: Belinda So
Food Editor: Christine Osmond
Production: Joan Beal

Text copyright © Jennifer Joyce 20101
The moral right of the author has been asserted.
Design copyright © Murdoch Books Pty Limited 2011
Illustrations copyright © Megan Hess 2011
Photography copyright © Maja Smend 2011

National Library of Australia Cataloguing-in-Publication Data
Author: Joyce, Jennifer
Title: Skinny Meals in Heels / Jennifer Joyce
ISBN: 978-1-74266-100-1 (hbk.)
Notes: Includes index.
Subjects: Cooking.
Dewey Number: 641.5

A catalogue record for this book is available from the British Library.

Printed by 1010 Printing International Limited, China.
Reprinted in 2012

IMPORTANT: Those who might be at risk from the effects of salmonella poisoning (the elderly, pregnant women,
young children and those suffering from immune deficiency diseases) should consult their doctor with any concerns
about eating raw eggs.

OVEN GUIDE: You may find cooking times vary depending on the oven you are using. For fan-forced ovens, as a
general rule, set the oven temperature to 20°C (35°F) lower than indicated in the recipe.